Soccer School

Name: ....

Class: ....

Coaches: ....

kickito ERgo SUM

To Maya, midfield marvel

A. B.

To ABC, with love

B. L.

Text copyright © 2016 by Alex Bellos and Ben Lyttleton
Illustrations copyright © 2016 by Spike Gerrell

First U.S. edition 2018

Library of Congress Catalog Card Number pending
ISBN 978-1-5362-0435-3

18 19 20 21 22 23 LSC 10 9 8 7 6 5 4 3 2 1

Printed in Crawfordsville, IN, U.S.A.

This book was typeset in Palatino.
The illustrations were done in ink with digital manipulation.

Walker Books
a division of
Candlewick Press
99 Dover Street
Somerville, Massachusetts 02144

www.walkerbooks.com

S⚽CCER SCHOOL

WHERE SOCCER ~~EXPLAINS~~ THE WORLD
RULES

Season 1

WALKER BOOKS

ALEX BELLOS & BEN LYTTLETON

illustrated by Spike Gerrell

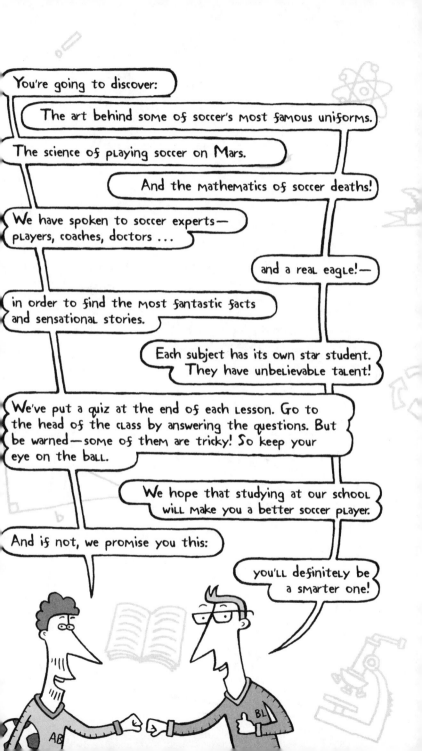

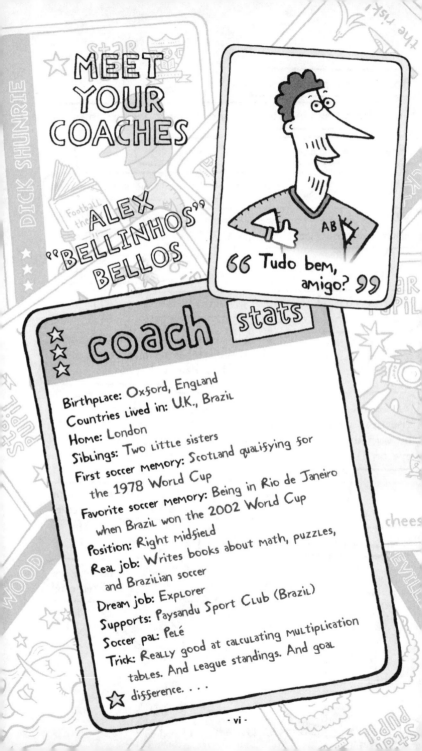

MEET YOUR COACHES

ALEX "BELLINHOS" BELLOS

66 Tudo bem, amigo? 99

☆☆☆ COACH stats

Birthplace: Oxford, England
Countries lived in: U.K., Brazil
Home: London
Siblings: Two little sisters
First soccer memory: Scotland qualifying for the 1978 World Cup
Favorite soccer memory: Being in Rio de Janeiro when Brazil won the 2002 World Cup
Position: Right midfield
Real job: Writes books about math, puzzles, and Brazilian soccer
Dream job: Explorer
Supports: Paysandu Sport Club (Brazil)
Soccer pal: Pelé
Trick: Really good at calculating multiplication tables. And league standings. And goal difference. . . .

coach stats

Birthplace: London
Home: London
Siblings: One older brother
First soccer memory: Finishing my first soccer sticker book in 1981
Greatest soccer moment: Scoring a penalty kick in front of 25,000 fans
Favorite uniform: Roma away, 2014–2015
Position: Left midfield
Real job: Soccer writer and pundit. Also a penalty-kick expert
Dream job: Soccer player
Supports: Littleton FC (Midland League Division One)
Soccer pal: Antonin Panenka
Trick: Never misses a penalty kick

BEN "THE PEN" LYTTLETON

66 Penalty, ref! 99

CLASS SCHEDULE

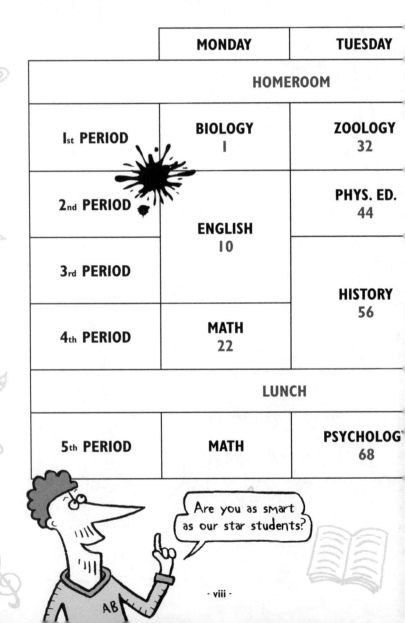

	MONDAY	**TUESDAY**
HOMEROOM		
1st PERIOD	**BIOLOGY** 1	**ZOOLOGY** 32
2nd PERIOD	**ENGLISH** 10	**PHYS. ED.** 44
3rd PERIOD		**HISTORY** 56
4th PERIOD	**MATH** 22	
LUNCH		
5th PERIOD	**MATH**	**PSYCHOLOGY** 68

Are you as smart as our star students?

WEDNESDAY	THURSDAY	FRIDAY
8:30–8:40 AM		
DESIGN TECHNOLOGY 78	PHOTOGRAPHY 122	POLITICAL SCIENCE 164
	BUSINESS STUDIES 134	
GEOGRAPHY 88	FASHION 144	MUSIC 176
DRAMA 100		
1:00–2:00 PM		
PHILOSOPHY 110	COMPUTER SCIENCE 154	PHYSICS 186

Find the answers to the quizzes on page 196. But no cheating!

Welcome to the first lesson of the week at Soccer School. We're going to begin with the super—and stinky!—subject of poop.

Professional soccer players take their digestive systems very seriously. Not only do they need to eat the right food so they stay fit and healthy; they also need to think about their poop. No one wants to have to go in the middle of a game, as you can't rush to the toilet with fifty thousand fans watching you. So top players plan when to go to the bathroom.

FARE PLAY

There are two parts to planning a poop. You need to eat the right food, and you need to eat it at the right time. Soccer players have special food doctors—called nutritionists—who make sure they eat properly. Here are two main meals often served before a game:

Chicken with boiled potatoes and carrots

Fish with rice and broccoli

And here are two meals that would never be served before a game:

Double cheeseburger and extra fries

Doughnuts

Food gives you the energy and the nutrients you need to survive. Potatoes and rice are served before games because they contain lots of carbohydrates, which give you energy. Since you need lots of energy to run around for ninety minutes chasing a ball, soccer players will have extra-large helpings of potatoes and rice.

Soccer players also eat lots of chicken and fish because they are packed with protein, which helps your body's cells grow and repair.

Vegetables like carrots and broccoli are a source of minerals and vitamins. These help boost your body's immune system, which protects you from infection or illness.

Cheeseburgers, fries, and doughnuts are full of fat. You don't want fat before a game because it causes the digestive system to slow down. The food sits in your stomach, making you feel full and heavy, which isn't good if you have to run around.

TOILET TIMINGS

In order to perfectly time a poop, you need to plan when you eat. Teams make sure their players eat a meal THREE HOURS before a game. This allows plenty of time for the food to pass through the digestive system.

The digestive system is the part of your body that takes in food, breaks it down, absorbs the nutrients, and, last but not least, makes poop.

The journey starts with food entering the **mouth**. After you give it a good chew, the mashed-up food plummets down a long tube, called the **esophagus**, to the **stomach**. There it is churned around, and chemicals in the stomach break down the food, with the help of other organs such as the **liver** and **pancreas**. The final stage is the **small** and **large intestines**, where the nutrients are absorbed into the blood and what remains is expelled through

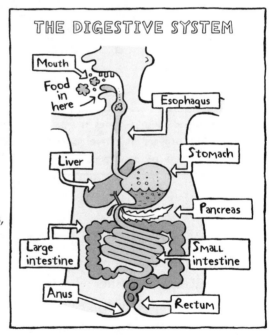

your **rectum** and **anus** (your butt) as poop. In an adult, the combined esophagus, stomach, and intestines—what we call our gut, or **alimentary canal**—is about thirty feet long.

GET IT ALL OUT

By kickoff time, a soccer player's meal will have completely broken down and any waste food will be ready to poop out. On one of the biggest teams in the English Premier League, there is a secret, malodorous ritual before a game starts. The players have a pooping procedure. They go to the toilet stalls in a predetermined order, partly based on seniority on the team. The most senior person poops first—for obvious, smell-related reasons!
Then, with empty stomachs, they are all ready for the game.

But it can be difficult to fix mealtimes (and pooping times) for players, because kickoff times are spread throughout the day. Weekend kickoffs are at lunchtime or in the afternoon, and midweek kickoffs are in the evening.

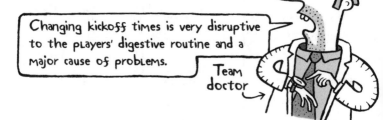

Changing kickoff times is very disruptive to the players' digestive routine and a major cause of problems.

Team doctor →

TUMMY TERROR

There's another reason why players tend to poop just before games, no matter what food they have eaten: fear.

When you get really, really scared, you want to poop. And just before a big match, a player will be full of fear. They will be scared of playing badly and losing.

Fear triggers funny feelings in our belly because of a built-in survival system common to all animals. Imagine you are an animal minding your own business and suddenly another, bigger, nasty-looking animal appears in your path. You need to make an instant decision about whether to fight it or to run away. In either case—fight or flight—your muscles must be ready, so the body will start diverting blood to them.

Whenever humans sense danger and get scared, like a soccer player before a game or a student before an exam, we respond in the same way. Blood is diverted to our muscles, we produce a chemical called adrenaline, and the chemistry of our body is altered, making it feel extra sensitive. This also causes tension in our gut, which is what gives us that butterfly sensation and can make us flee . . . to the toilet.

Remember, anyone can get butterflies in the stomach— even the most famous players in the world. And sometimes, despite all this pre-match planning, pooping can still go wrong.

The manager said it would be good to have some butterflies in my tummy.

HAVE WE GOT POOS FOR YOU

WIPE

Gary Lineker was one of England's best-ever strikers. At the 1986 World Cup, he scored six goals and won the prize, known as the Golden Boot, for top scorer. But the 1990 World Cup started quite, well, poo-rly for him. "I tried to tackle someone, stretched and relaxed myself, and er . . ." Lineker said of the moment he pooped himself on the field against the Republic of Ireland in England's first game of the tournament. "I was not very well. I was poorly at halftime. I was very fortunate that it rained that night so I could do something about it, but it was messy. You can see me rubbing the ground like a dog trying to clean itself. It was the most horrendous experience of my life." There was some good news: the Irish players did not want to get too close to him. "I have never found so much space after that in my life," he said, laughing.

 FOUL

Mexico was 1–1 with local rivals the USA in 2011, and there were just a few minutes left to play when Mexican midfielder Omar Arellano bent down to adjust his socks. As the TV cameras zoomed in for a close-up, there was a surprise for viewers: a suspicious-looking brown stain

on the back of his white shorts, which was shown around the world.

YUCK

"I was on two courses of antibiotics at the time for a kick on my leg, which resulted in an upset stomach," said Welsh midfielder Robbie Savage about the day his Leicester City team played Aston Villa in the English Premier League in April 2002. "I had a bad case of diarrhea on the day of the game, so had to go there and then, and the nearest place was the referee's toilet." It was an expensive decision: the referee, Graham Poll, reported him for "improper conduct," and Savage had to pay a fine.

CHEEK

English winger Jason Puncheon ran off the field in the middle of the second half during an English Premier League game for Southampton against Everton in 2013. He returned a few minutes later with a grin on his face and the fans chanting a song that suggested he had gone for a poop. Puncheon appeared to confirm their suspicions when he celebrated scoring his next goal a couple of weeks later: he ran to the corner flag, bent down, and pretended to wipe his butt.

DOGGIE DOO

Soccer is not the only sport where poop is better out than in. In greyhound racing, it is said that the dog who poops just before the start will win the race. Fans like to keep a close eye on the dogs just in case any of them start to squat. . . .

TOMMY ACHE

STAR STUDENT

66 It wasn't me! 99

STAR STUDENT stats

Favorite number: 2
Daily intake of prunes: 25
Butterflies in stomach: 324
Underpants worn under shorts: 3
Birthplace: Crapstone, England
Supports: Arsenal (U.K.)
Fave player: Kaká
Trick: Smelling danger

BIOLOGY QUIZ

1. Which of the following is NOT part of the digestive system?

a) Esophagus
b) Stomach
c) Liver
d) Nose

2. If an adult stretched out his or her intestines, they would be as long as:

a) the height of a goalpost.
b) the width of a goal.
c) the width of a soccer field.
d) the distance from the center circle to the nearest toilet.

3. How many times will a person fart on average every 100 minutes?

a) 0 times
b) 1 time
c) 10 times
d) 100 times

4. What was Brazilian striker Ronaldo caught doing while playing in a game at the 1996 Olympic Games?

a) Eating his booger
b) Farting in an opponent's face
c) Peeing out of the side of his shorts
d) Burping at the referee

5. Wembley Stadium in London has more bathrooms than any other stadium in the world. How many does it have?

a) 418
b) 818
c) 1,318
d) 2,618

This lesson is about the language of soccer. In order to enjoy the game, you need to be able to talk the talk. Can you tell the difference between a howler and a screamer? No, it's not about the noise they make.

Soccer language is famous for its **clichés**, which are expressions that are used so often, they become completely unoriginal things to say. An example is "It's a funny old game." You may have spotted a few others in our cartoon.

Today we are looking at the *ABCD*, which is short for *Alex and Ben's Classroom Dictionary*. It is full of soccer **jargon**, which is the special language that is not understood by outsiders. We explain some of the intriguing origins of these words and phrases. The vocabulary will help you understand the game at a deeper level. It will also mean that when you listen to commentators or professional players, you will be able to understand the words they are using— even if they are talking nonsense, which they often are!

- 11 -

Alex and Ben's Classroom Dictionary

4-4-2 • a tactical formation that refers to four defenders, four midfielders, and two attacking players in the starting eleven. Goalkeepers are not mentioned, as everyone knows they are there. 4-4-2 has traditionally been the most common formation in American soccer, although today's teams often play with four defenders, two defensive midfielders, three attacking midfielders, and one center forward. This formation is called a 4-2-3-1. ⚽

the beautiful game • a phrase often used to describe soccer. It's an English translation of the Portuguese phrase *o jogo bonito,* which was made famous by Alex's soccer pal, the Brazilian player Pelé. ○ ◉

bicycle kick • a kick in which the player jumps and swings one foot to kick the ball over their head while their body is horizontal. At the moment of the kick, it looks like the player is riding an imaginary bicycle in the air. The bicycle kick is not to be confused with the overhead kick, which is when the player hangs vertically upside down to kick the ball. 👟

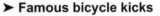

Key players

➤ Famous bicycle kicks

Mark Hughes
(**Wales** vs. Spain, 1985)
Jean-Pierre Papin
(**France** vs. Belgium, 1992)
Peter Crouch
(**Liverpool** vs. Galatasaray, 2006)
Wayne Rooney
(**Manchester United** vs. Manchester City, 2011)
Lisa De Vanna
(**Sky Blue** vs. Boston Breakers, 2013)

Key | ⚽ = **tactic** | 👟 = **technique** | ○ = **jargon** | ◉ = **origin**

bogey team • *Bogey* is an old word for a ghost, goblin, or evil spirit. A bogey team is one you always lose to or that brings you bad luck. In golf, the word is also linked to bad luck: a bogey is a score of one more than the expected score, or par, for a hole.

🔈

brace • When two goals are scored by the same player in the same match, it is called a brace. This comes from the French word for arms (*bras*), of which we have two.

🔈 🎙

catenaccio • a system of defensive play invented in Italy that uses an extra player behind the defense to ensure that all attacks on the goal are blocked. When the strategy works, the attacking side cannot get through. *Catenaccio* is Italian for "door bolt."

⚽ 🎙

(El) Clásico • most commonly used to mean a match between Spanish teams Real Madrid and Barcelona. It can also mean any game between two rival teams, usually from the same area, in Spanish-speaking countries, such as Argentina or Mexico.

🎙 🔈

derby • a game between two teams from the same area. The word comes from the 12th earl of Derby, who founded a famous horse race in 1780 at Epsom, near London, which is still held every year. It's where the Kentucky Derby got its name. The term *derby* came to be used in England for any big sports event, and then for an important event between two local teams.

🎙

Alex and Ben's Classroom Dictionary

drubbing • a resounding defeat, such as the game in 2002 when Stade Olympique L'Emyrne (SOE), the previous season's champions of Madagascar, lost 149–0 to rival AS Adema. The game holds the world record for the highest score in professional soccer. Even though SOE lost the game, they scored all 149 goals. This is because they were all own goals scored in protest at refereeing decisions that had gone against them in previous games. The SOE coach was banned from soccer for three years after the game. ○

dugout • the bench or benches where the coach and substitutes sit during a match. It used to be dug out of the ground but usually isn't anymore. ○

fair-weather fan • a fan who supports a team only when the team is doing well. The

Stats and facts

➤ Famous derbies

COUNTRY	RIVAL TEAMS	NAME OF DERBY
England	Manchester United vs. Liverpool	North-west Derby
France	Paris Saint-Germain vs. Marseille	Le Classique
Germany	Borussia Dortmund vs. Bayern Munich	Der Klassiker
Italy	Inter Milan vs. Juventus	Derby d'Italia
Portugal	Benfica vs. Porto	O Clássico
Spain	Real Madrid vs. Barcelona	El Clásico

➤ Famous drubbings

YEAR	COUNTRY	WINNERS	LOSERS	SCORE
1885	Scotland	Arbroath	Bon Accord	36–0
1971	Tahiti	Tahiti	Cook Islands	30–0
2001	Australia	Australia	American Samoa	31–0
2013	Nigeria	Plateau United Feeders	Akurba	79–0

Key | ☉ = tactic | 👊 = technique | ○ = jargon | ⚲ = origin

comparison is to a person who goes outside in good weather but stays indoors when the weather is bad. So a fair-weather fan stops supporting a team when they are losing. ○

galáctico • (*"galactic"* in Spanish) Originally a name for the star players recruited by Real Madrid, this term is now used to describe the most famous international players. It refers to a player who is so good, they seem to come from another galaxy. ℚ

group of death • a group in the first stages of a competition with so many strong teams that at least one of them will be knocked out early. ○

hat trick • when three goals are scored by the same player in the same match. The term dates back to 1858 and is from the traditional English sport of cricket, a version of baseball that takes much longer. H. H. Stephenson, playing the pitcher role, struck out three opponents in three

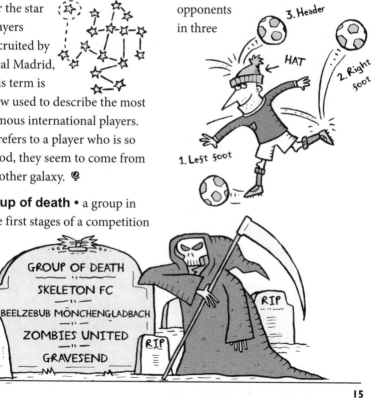

3. Header

HAT

2. Right foot

1. Left foot

GROUP OF DEATH
"
SKELETON FC
"
BEELZEBUB MÖNCHENGLADBACH
"
ZOMBIES UNITED
"
GRAVESEND

RIP

RIP

consecutive throws, and fans were so impressed, they collected money and bought him a hat. The phrase "hat trick" caught on and became used in other sports, including ice hockey. The perfect hat trick in soccer consists of one goal scored with the left foot, one with the right foot, and one with the head. ○ ◉

magic sponge • used by team doctors to treat players when they are lying on the field injured. It's just a normal sponge with no real magic powers, but often a splash of cold water can help hurt players recover. Cold water reduces the blood supply to the injured area, preventing swelling and allowing the players to get back into the game. That's why the sponge is seen as magical. ○

−30°C

Matildas • the nickname for the Australian national women's team, after "Waltzing Matilda," the most famous song in Australia and the country's unofficial national anthem. ○ ◉

nutmeg • To nutmeg means to pass the ball through an opponent's legs. The origin of the verb is not known, although several derivations have been suggested: **1.** The word *nutmeg* is Cockney rhyming slang for leg. **2.** The nutmeg is a reference to the "nuts," or testicles, of the player between whose legs the ball is passed. **3.** In the nineteenth century, the phrase "to be nutmegged" meant "to be deceived,"

Key | ☻ = tactic | 👆 = technique | ○ = jargon | ◉ = origin since nutmegs were very expensive and often sellers conned people by adding wooden nuts into bags of nutmegs. 👋 💭 🔍

parking the bus • when almost all the players on a team stay on defense. This has the same effect as parking the team bus in front of their goal. ⚽ 💭

poacher • In soccer, a poacher is a striker who loiters around the goal area and is particularly lethal at scoring from fleeting chances. (A poacher is someone who goes hunting in places where they are not allowed to.) ⚽ 💭

Stats and facts

➤ Anyone for nutmeg?

Other countries have their own unique words and phrases to describe the act of kicking a ball between a player's legs.

LANGUAGE	TERM
Arabic (Egypt, Jordan, Syria)	egg
Austrian	gherkin
Danish	tunnel
Dutch	gate
Finnish	collar
French	little bridge
German	tunnel
Hebrew	to thread a needle
Italian	tunnel
Korean	to hatch an egg
Portuguese (Brazil)	pen
Spanish (Latin America)	spout
Swedish	tunnel
Turkish	cradle

promotion/relegation • the system used in all European soccer leagues by which teams are rewarded for good or bad performances over the length of a season. **Promotion** is the movement of a team that finishes at or near the top of the standings to the higher division, while **relegation** is the demotion of a team at or near the bottom to the league below. ○

rabona • a "crossed" kick, in which the kicking foot goes around the back of the standing leg, thus making the legs cross. In 1948, the Argentinian player Ricardo Infante scored the earliest recorded goal like this— from 35 yards out. When reporting on the game, a local sports magazine wanted to get across the cheekiness of the move, so it said that Infante—whose name means "child" in Spanish —was doing a *rabona*, meaning he was skipping school. The name stuck. 🎤 ✋

shutout • when a team doesn't let in any goals in a game. In the U.K., this is known as a "clean sheet." ○

six-pointer • a game between two teams who are neck-and-neck in the league standings, usually toward the end of the season and when the teams are in the running for promotion or relegation. In standings, game winners get three points and losers get no points. When the teams are neck and neck, however, not only do the winners get three points, but losers are also denied the three points that they could have gotten had they been playing another team. The three points gained plus the three points denied add up to six points. ○

Key players

➤ **Rabona experts**

Eden Hazard
Erik Lamela
Ángel Di María
Neymar
Cristiano Ronaldo

Key | ☻ = tactic | ✋ = technique | ○ = jargon | 🎤 = origin

square ball • when a ball is passed sideways, rather than forward or backward. (Not a ball that isn't round.)

stepover • a trick in which the player moves their foot over the ball without touching it, so as to fool the opposing player into thinking that they are moving with the ball in that direction. Pedro Calomino, an Argentinian player for Boca Juniors in the early twentieth century, is believed to have invented it.

supersub • a substitute who often wins games by scoring a crucial late goal. Some strikers are experts at coming onto the field and finding space when defenders are tired.

tiki-taka • a style of soccer, developed at Barcelona, in which the players make lots of short passes and maintain possession for long periods.

vuvuzela • a plastic horn that makes a very loud noise when you blow it, and which was used by fans at the 2010 World Cup, in South Africa.

Key players

➤ Supersub kings

Roger Milla (Cameroon, 1973–1994)
David Fairclough (Liverpool, 1975–1983)
Ole Gunnar Solskjær (Manchester United, 1996–2007)
Henrik Larsson (Barcelona, 2004–2006)
Mohamed Nagy (Egypt, 2009–)

KICK-TIONARY CORNER

The nine words below can be used for different types of kicks, from a terrible one (howler) to a brilliant one (screamer). Can you think of any others?

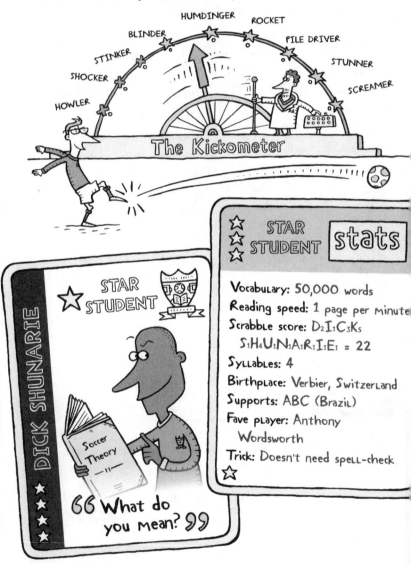

HUMDINGER
ROCKET
BLINDER
PILE DRIVER
STINKER
STUNNER
SHOCKER
SCREAMER
HOWLER

The Kickometer

☆
☆☆ STAR
☆☆☆ STUDENT stats

Vocabulary: 50,000 words
Reading speed: 1 page per minute
Scrabble score: $D_2 I_1 C_3 K_5$
$S_1 H_4 U_1 N_1 A_1 R_1 I_1 E_1 = 22$
Syllables: 4
Birthplace: Verbier, Switzerland
Supports: ABC (Brazil)
Fave player: Anthony Wordsworth
Trick: Doesn't need spell-check
☆

DICK SHUNARIE

☆ STAR STUDENT

Soccer Theory

66 What do you mean? 99

ENGLISH QUIZ

1. Which of the following clichés is NOT used for scoring a goal?

a) Finding the back of the net
b) Beating the keeper
c) Rattling the woodwork
d) Slamming it home

2. Which is the correct cliché? The striker leaped like a:

a) Giraffe
b) Kangaroo
c) Flea
d) Salmon

3. What is a banana kick?

a) A goal scored by a player in yellow cleats
b) A pass or shot that curls
c) A goalkeeper's kick that goes so high, monkeys in trees could catch it
d) A kick that causes the player to slip on the field

4. What is a Christmas-tree formation?

a) A tradition in Lapland in which the league leader at Christmas gives presents to opposition fans
b) A pile of dirty cleats that look like presents at the bottom of a tree
c) A tactical system of 4-3-2-1, which, when viewed from above, has the shape of a Christmas tree
d) The league standings on December 25

5. What is the name of the ripple effect that goes around a stadium when fans stand up with their hands in the air and then sit down again?

a) Riptide
b) Surf
c) Wave
d) Jumping fish

Get your calculators out! In this lesson we're doing some math problems.

We're going to figure out the risk of dying during a game of soccer—because some really unlucky things could happen to you on the field.

You could be struck by lightning.

You could be whacked by a falling crossbar.

You could collide with a wall by the side of the field.

You could score a goal, celebrate by somersaulting in the air, land badly, and break your back.

Soccer players have died in all these circumstances. :-(We don't want any of you to die at Soccer School, so we're going to find out how dangerous soccer really is. We'll also discover what is the greatest health risk to players and what's being done about it.

But just to be safe: don't play during lightning storms; check the crossbar; don't run into walls; and practice your somersaults.

Our striker is deadly.

Well, dead, anyway.

KAPOW!!!

WHAT ARE THE CHANCES?

In order to calculate the risk of dying while playing soccer, we need to count all the people who have died playing soccer and divide this number by the total number of people who have ever played soccer.

Because this is math, we can write this as an **equation**:

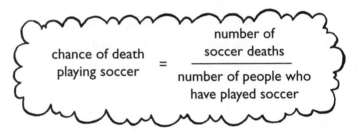

$$\text{chance of death playing soccer} = \frac{\text{number of soccer deaths}}{\text{number of people who have played soccer}}$$

Easy! Well, not quite. It is impossible to know all the people who have ever died playing soccer, since no one has kept a list.

However, a university in Germany counted all the people in one city who died playing sports over a ten-year period. We are going to use this data to calculate the annual risk of a person dying during a game of soccer.

The table below shows the number of deaths from different sports in Hamburg, a city with a population of 1.7 million, between 1997 and 2006. Ping-Pong had the fewest deaths, swimming the most, and soccer is in the middle.

SPORT	NUMBER OF DEATHS BETWEEN 1997 AND 2006, INCLUSIVE
Ping-Pong	7
Horseback riding	10
Tennis	15
Soccer	17
Running	18
Cycling	19
Swimming	31

To calculate the chances of dying while playing soccer in Hamburg, we need to divide 17—the number of soccer deaths—by the total number of people in Hamburg who played soccer in that ten-year period.

But how do we find out how many Hamburgers played soccer? According to FIFA, the international governing body for professional soccer, one-fifth of the total population of Germany plays soccer. We can therefore assume that one-fifth of the population of Hamburg played soccer during that time. That's one-fifth of 1.7 million, which is:

$$1,700,000 \div 5 = 340,000$$

Now we can return to the equation and do our calculation.

In Hamburg for the period between 1997 and 2006, we can say that:

$$\text{chance of death playing soccer} = \frac{\text{number of soccer deaths}}{\text{number of people who have played soccer}} = \frac{17}{340,000}$$

When we divide top and bottom by 17, we get:

$$= \frac{1}{20,000} \text{ or } 1 \text{ in } 20,000$$

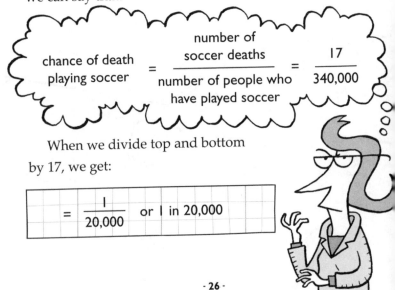

So, in the ten years from 1997 to 2006, one person in 20,000 died in Hamburg playing soccer. We want to find the chance of dying in a single year, which is going to be one-tenth the chance of dying over ten years. One tenth of $1/20,000$ is $1/10 \times 1/20,000 = 1/200,000$, or 1 in 200,000.

We have our answer! We've calculated that between 1997 and 2006, the annual chance of dying while playing a game of soccer in Hamburg was about 1 in 200,000.

We can assume that the number has stayed about the same, because it wasn't long ago. And since the lifestyle in Hamburg is similar to that in the United States, we can generalize and say that the annual chance of death playing soccer in the United States is probably also about 1 in 200,000.

But that's not *your* chance of dying while playing soccer. The 1 in 200,000 figure applies to all people: young and old, professional and amateur, fat and thin. The Hamburg study found that most soccer deaths were from heart attacks. Those most at risk were out-of-shape adults, whose hearts were not able to take the pressure of vigorous exercise. If you are young and healthy, the risk of dying from a heart attack while playing soccer is very, very small.

And the risk of being hit by a lightning strike or a crossbar falling on your head is even smaller.

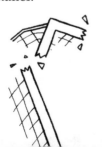

BROKEN HEART

In rare cases, professional players have suffered from a weak heart. In 2003, midfielder Marc-Vivien Foé collapsed and died while playing for Cameroon against Colombia in the Confederations Cup semifinal. It turned out that Foé had a type of heart disease that had gone undetected all his life.

As a result of Foé's death, FIFA introduced safety procedures to try to make sure no professional died from an undetected heart condition ever again. In the professional leagues, players are now screened for heart disease before tournaments. Stadiums must have **defibrillators**, which are machines used on people who have had heart attacks. They deliver electric shocks through the chest that can return the heart to a normal rhythm.

These new procedures have already saved a life.

In 2012, Bolton Wanderers midfielder Fabrice Muamba was playing an FA Cup match, the championship game of the English Football—or soccer—Association, against Tottenham Hotspur. After forty-three minutes, he suddenly fell to the ground. His heart had stopped beating. This is called a **cardiac arrest** and happens when the heart stops pumping blood through the body. He was twenty-three years old.

Medical staff hurried to help Muamba and gave him **cardiopulmonary resuscitation**, known as CPR, pumping his chest to artificially keep oxygen flowing through his body. The team also used the stadium's defibrillators. Muamba's heart did not beat for seventy-eight minutes before it started working properly again. One Hotspurs fan who was at the game, Dr. Andrew Deaner, rushed onto the field to help and then treated Muamba at the London Chest Hospital, where he worked. Muamba thanked Deaner, and everyone was happy about the result—even the Spurs fans.

LET'S HAVE SUM FUN

There are safer ways of talking about math at Soccer School. Alex developed his love of numbers when he was at school by looking at league standings and figuring out the goal difference between teams.

That was taken one step further in Romania, when the national team had fun with their shirt numbers for a friendly match against Spain. The players wore math problems on their backs, and the answer was their normal shirt number. The player who usually wore 6 wore $2 + 2 + 2$. Player number 23 wore $46 \div 2$, and player number 14 was now 2×7. The head of Romanian soccer, Ben's friend Răzvan Burleanu, said they did it to give children a different way of discovering math. Răzvan has the right idea: he can come and teach math at Soccer School anytime.

IVÁN A LAUGH

Chilean striker Iván Zamorano took a page out of Romania's math book back in 1998. He lost his favorite shirt number to Brazilian teammate Ronaldo when they both played for the Italian team Inter Milan. Ronaldo was given the number 9 shirt, but Zamorano wanted to keep his number, so he wore 18 but made the uniform designers add a little plus sign between the numbers—as in $1 + 8 = 9$. Good thinking, Iván!

STAR STUDENT stats

Broken bones: 24
Hospital visits: 312
Annual bandage budget: $2,500
Favorite number: 911
Birthplace: Providence, Rhode Island
Supports: San Jose Earthquakes (United States)
Fave player: Luis Boa Morte (whose surname is Portuguese for "good death")
☆ Trick: Parachutes onto field ✚

STAR STUDENT

LUCKY S. CAPES

"Take the risk!"

MATH QUIZ

1. **Which sport causes the most deaths, according to research mentioned in the lesson?**

a) Swimming
b) Running
c) Horseback riding
d) Ping-Pong

2. **If the chances of something happening are 4 in 20, this is the same as:**

a) 1 in 3
b) 1 in 4
c) 1 in 5
d) 1 in 20

3. **Why does Italian striker Mario Balotelli currently wear the number 9 shirt?**

a) He changes his hairstyle nine times a year.
b) He scored nine goals in his first game as a professional.
c) He wanted to wear number 45, and 4 + 5 = 9.
d) He was born in 2009.

4. **What shirt number was Moroccan striker Hicham Zerouali allowed to wear when he played for Scottish team Aberdeen in 2000?**

a) 0
b) 1
c) 1000
d) Infinity

5. **What did the referee do when Croatian defender Goran Tunjic collapsed after a heart attack in a fifth-division game in 2010?**

a) He gave him mouth-to-mouth resuscitation.
b) He cautioned him for diving.
c) He asked if there were any doctors in the crowd.
d) He carried him off the field and waved "Play on."

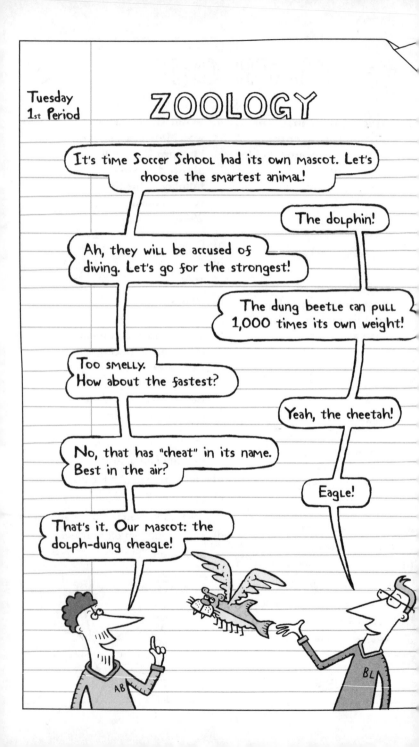

Enough about death! Here at Soccer School, we prefer life in all its manifestations—especially animals. Ben has a pet dog he runs with every day in the park. Alex doesn't have a pet but scratches his back like a monkey.

In this lesson, we'll talk about teams and their animal mascots, which are the animals that fans believe symbolize their team and bring them good luck. We are interested only in real, live animals, not those mascots that are just giant costumes with people inside them. Many teams have live-animal mascots. Their job is a risky one, as we will see. Giddy up!

GOOOAAAAAAAAAT

A goat wearing a snazzy red cloak trots into the stadium of German team Cologne. Fans cheer and take pictures. The glamorous mammal is Hennes VIII, Cologne's mascot, who watches every home game from the same patch of grass by a corner flag.

Hennes is the most famous goat in Germany. In fact, he's the only famous goat in Germany!

Hennes is a billy goat, which is the name for a male goat. (Females are called nanny goats.) In Europe, farmers mainly keep goats for their milk, which is then turned into cheese. But in parts of Africa, Asia, and the Caribbean, goat meat is often on the menu—don't tell Hennes!

During games, Hennes stands next to his handler, Ingo Reipka, who keeps him on a short leather leash. The goat munches on carrots and bread and even finds the field tasty. "Sometimes he eats the grass—the only thing he doesn't like is the white lines," says Reipka. Hennes gets a bit restless when the linesman runs past him, and he doesn't really like it when the action comes his way, because he is afraid of the ball.

On one occasion, Nigerian striker Anthony Ujah got in trouble over Hennes. After scoring a goal for Cologne, he ran to where Hennes was standing and pulled his horns. Ouch! Reipka had to calm the billy goat down. Ujah later said, "Apologies to Hennes for my hard celebration."

The goat is called Hennes VIII because he is the eighth goat named Hennes to occupy the role of Cologne mascot. It is said that the tradition started in 1950, when a circus owner gave a billy goat to the club as a lucky charm. They named him after Hennes Weisweiler, who was the Cologne coach at the time.

Goats have a life span of only about fifteen years, so when Hennes died, he was replaced by Hennes II, and so on until Hennes VIII became the mascot in 2008 after an online vote among fans to choose from four candidates.

The most famous of Cologne's goats was Hennes VII. He even appeared in TV shows, including once as a murder victim in a German crime drama. Hennes used to travel with the players on the team bus, but it's safer for his handler to take him to games on his own. Hennes VIII now lives in a log cabin in Cologne Zoo, which he shares with Anneliese, his favorite nanny goat. The cabin has a fireplace filled with hay, and the walls are covered with Cologne flags and photos.

The Hennes tradition became so popular with the team that he is now on their team logo, and Cologne is known in Germany as the Billy Goats.

A legendary goatherd from Ethiopia named Kaldi is said to have discovered the coffee plant when he saw his goats dancing after they nibbled the plant's berries.

Scientists say that some goats' accents change to fit their surroundings when they move away from their family.

Cashmere is a super-soft wool produced by cashmere goats. It got its name because it was first made in a region in South Asia called Kashmir.

Goat Facts

YOU HAVE GOAT TO BE KIDDING ME

Cologne is not the only soccer team with a horned history. More than a hundred years ago, the English team Manchester United had a goat as a mascot. In 1906, the director of Benson's, a traveling theater troupe, gave defender Charlie Roberts a goat named

Billy. No one knows why. A dog named Major had been United's mascot, but Billy took over its duties. Before every game, he was paraded around the field. After some games, Billy even went with the players to the local bar and toasted wins with a little drink.

Billy's last game was the 1909 FA Cup final, when Manchester United beat Bristol City 1–0. He joined the Manchester United players celebrating after the game, but he died of suspected alcohol poisoning soon after. It was thought that he had drunk too much beer or champagne. That was the last time Manchester United had a live animal as a mascot. *Hic!*

OWL ABOUT THAT?

As Billy proved, being a mascot can be a dangerous job. In 2011, a Colombian league game turned ugly after Panamanian defender Luis Moreno was accused by opposition fans of "murdering" an owl during a match. The owl, who lived in the stadium roof, was the mascot of

the Barranquilla side Atlético Junior. He had been hit by the ball and was lying on the field with an injured leg. Moreno, apparently eager for the game to continue, was seen to kick the owl toward the sideline with his left foot.

Fans chanted "Murderer!" at the player. Vets were later unable to save the owl's life. Moreno apologized "to the entire Colombian country" and was given a lecture about owls at his local zoo. He promised to return to the zoo once a month to help out.

Lots of owl species have asymmetrical ears—of different sizes and at different positions on their heads.

Owls have three eyelids: one for blinking, one for sleeping, and one for keeping the eye clean and healthy.

All owls hoot, but some make other noises too. The barn owl hisses when it is scared.

EAGLES HAVE LANDED

Speaking of birds, did you know the most common animal mascot for soccer teams is the eagle?

The eagle, in fact, has been a symbol of strength, superiority, and courage since ancient times, because of its awesome fighting skills and beautiful appearance.

Eagles are birds of prey, which means that they kill and eat other animals. Usually they go for small mammals like rabbits and mice, but they can even kill wolves and foxes.

Eagles are speedy birds. They can fly at up to 55 miles / 88.5 kilometers per hour and can dive at 100 miles / 160 kilometers per hour.

Their eyesight is incredible too. We have eyes on the front of our face and so can see only forward, but eagles have eyes on the sides of their head, so they can see forward, to the sides, and (almost) behind themselves. On top of this, their eyesight is around four times better than ours. They can spot a rabbit from a mile away. That's why when someone is very observant we call them "eagle-eyed."

One expert told us that the eagle's beaked face makes it look majestic. No wonder that throughout history the eagle has been called the "king of the skies."

This team is of a high standard!

SPQR

EAGLES

REGAL EAGLES

In ancient Rome, the eagle represented power, freedom, wisdom, and nobility. Every unit of soldiers in an ancient Roman army had an eagle **standard**, or flag, which was the military equivalent of a mascot. Losing the eagle standard would represent defeat for the army.

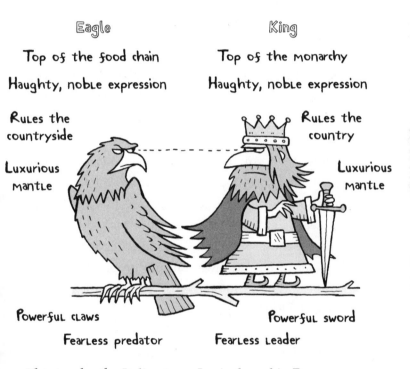

Eagle

Top of the food chain

Haughty, noble expression

Rules the countryside

Luxurious mantle

Powerful claws

Fearless predator

King

Top of the monarchy

Haughty, noble expression

Rules the country

Luxurious mantle

Powerful sword

Fearless leader

This is why the Italian team Lazio, based in Rome, has an eagle on its logo and flies a live eagle, called Olimpia, around the stadium before games. "The eagle is very important for us; it is our history," explained Lazio owner Claudio Lotito. Olimpia lives at the team training ground and receives regular visits from Lazio fans and players.

- 39 -

Ancient Rome's use of the eagle as a symbol of freedom spread around the world. In 1782, the United States adopted the bald eagle, which can be found only in North America, as its national bird.

In 1904, the Portuguese team Sport Lisboa, which later became Benfica, was one of the first teams to use the eagle as a sports emblem. Other teams followed suit. In 1973, English team Crystal Palace's manager, Malcolm Allison, changed the team's nickname from the Glaziers to the Eagles—because Benfica was one of Europe's best teams at the time and he admired them. Now lots of teams are known as the Eagles.

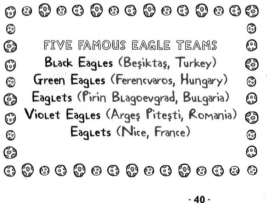

KAYLA THE EAGLE

Crystal Palace's nickname stuck, and the eagle was adopted as the team's mascot. In captivity, eagles can live fifty years. Kayla, the current Crystal Palace mascot, is in her mid-twenties, so has many more years of flying around the stadium before games and at half-time. Kayla was born in Canada, but in 2010 she moved to England and became the London team's mascot.

We will stop at nothing to find out fascinating facts for you, so we spoke to her handler, Alan Ames. He said that her full wingspan of seven feet is a very impressive sight, but you need to keep an eye on her: sometimes she will leave a poop-shaped present on opposition fans' heads. He told us that when Millwall fans chanted, "You're just a pigeon!" at her, she swooped down but was not quite able to snatch one fan's snack.

Ames says that crowds never stress Kayla out, but a strong wind does. Before one game, a powerful gust blew her above the roof of the stadium, and she was temporarily lost. Luckily she was wearing a tracking device, and her handler quickly found her.

She loves meeting fans, although she is not sure what to make of Palace's other eagle mascots, Pete and Alice, who are adults wearing eagle costumes. "She thinks they are jerks in silly clothes, and she mostly ignores them," said Ames. "She knows that she's the boss."

KAYLA SPEAKS

We even interviewed Kayla. (We had to use her handler, Alan Ames, as our interpreter, as he told us he speaks Eaglish.)

Favorite player?

The goalkeeper; he didn't drop me.

Favorite band?

Kings of Leon. I was on their album cover.

What do you think of humans?

Crazy. I only work for 8 minutes a day.

Favorite song?

"Eagles! Eagles!"

ROBYN BIRD

STAR STUDENT

66 I'm on the wing! 99

STAR STUDENT stats

Pets: 286
Number of legs on pets: 1,427 (includes Sammy the seven-legged spider)
Arm span: 5 ft./1.5 m
Highest whistle frequency: 46 kHz
Birthplace: Beaver, Alaska
Supports: Wolfsburg (Germany)
Favorite player: Chris Eagles
Trick: Predator in the box

ZOOLOGY QUIZ

1. Which of the following is a bird of prey?

a) Chicken
b) Flamingo
c) Eagle
d) Robin

2. What animal are all dogs descended from?

a) Wolf
b) Woolly mammoth
c) Rabbit
d) Fox

3. Three of these countries have an eagle on their national flag. The fourth has another kind of winged animal. Which country is it, and what's the animal?

a) Albania
b) Mexico
c) Wales
d) Egypt

4. What is the name of the Canadian team Toronto's flying mascot?

a) Bitchy the Hawk
b) Freddy the Falcon
c) Ticker the Rooster
d) Stolly the Squirrel

5. Which team is nicknamed the Monkey Hangers after people in their town hanged a monkey in the early 1800s because they thought it was a French spy?

a) Scunthorpe United
b) Hartlepool United
c) Crewe Alexandra
d) Plymouth Argyle

B L X O
F T I V

_ _ N G _ _ S

PHYSICAL EDUCATION

Are you an only child? Do you have brothers or sisters? If so, are you the oldest, youngest, or in the middle? And what on earth does this have to do with soccer? Quite a lot, actually.

This lesson is about the influence of our families on our soccer skills. Mom and Dad play a role, obviously—but so do brothers and sisters. It turns out that your chances of soccer glory are influenced by whether you were born first or last.

One final question: When is your birthday? This is also important to your soccer career. (And we want to send you a birthday card.)

SIBLING SUCCESS

Brothers and sisters can be really, really annoying. But here's the catch: if you want to be a professional soccer player, they can be really useful to have.

This is because chances are that when you want to kick a ball around, your siblings will be there to play with as ready-made teammates. And the more you practice, the better you will be.

Take the case of Paul Pogba, the French midfielder, and his twin older brothers, Florentin and Mathias. "I told Paul he was wasting his time playing with kids his own age, so he played with me and Mathias," said Florentin, who is two years older. "It was hard for him, but it built up his character. Sometimes he came home in tears because we were stronger than him, but it helped him improve."

Mathias added, "Paul, as the youngest, wanted to be like us. . . . We told him: 'Come and play with us, and your game will progress quicker. You'll become stronger.' Just look at him now. It worked." Eventually Paul became better than his brothers and one of the French team's most important players. Florentin and Mathias play for Guinea, the African country where their dad was born.

LITTLE TERRORS

As in the case of Paul Pogba, it is often really helpful to have siblings who are older than you, since you will be forced to play at their level. Some of the world's best strikers have older brothers or sisters.

PLAYER	OLDER SIBLINGS
Gareth Bale (Wales)	Vicky
Harry Kane (England)	Charlie
Marta (Brazil)	Angela, Valdir, and José
Lionel Messi (Argentina)	Rodrigo and Matías
Luis Suarez (Uruguay)	Paolo, Giovanna, and Leticia

Scientists have investigated the phenomenon of younger siblings doing better than older siblings in sports. Dr. Michael Perkin, an expert in child health at Saint George's Hospital in London, counted the number of oldest, middle, and youngest children among soccer players in one league in English soccer. He discovered that 46 percent—that's almost half—of the players surveyed were youngest children.

It really is an advantage being the baby in the family!

Research into other sports has shown that youngest children play in a different way from oldest children. For example, a study found that older children who play baseball feel more responsibility and don't take many risks, while youngest children make more risky decisions during play.

Only children 4%

Oldest children 28%

Middle children 22%

Youngest children 46%

Taking risks isn't good if you are a goalkeeper, but it can be a really useful thing if you are farther up the field. Sometimes taking risks can lead to scoring great goals.

Dr. Perkin made another discovery. He showed that the average number of siblings a player has changes depending on their position.

On average, if you have only one sibling, you're more likely to be in goal. And on the whole, attackers have more brothers and sisters than defenders do.

Goalkeepers
1.1 siblings

Defenders
1.8 siblings

Strikers
2.0 siblings

Midfielders
2.4 siblings

However, this doesn't always hold true.
Former France captain Patrice Evra has
twenty-four (yes, TWENTY-FOUR) brothers
and sisters. And yet he was a defender.
Imagine trying to brush your teeth in
the morning in a household
that size. . . .

FULL-TIME SCORE

| NATURE | 1 |
| NURTURE | 1 |

NATURE VS. NURTURE

So Big Bro and Big Sis can help you in your soccer career.
Most important, however, are Mom and Dad. They
influence you in two ways, whether you like it or not.

1. NATURE

Inside every cell in our body is a catalog of information—
our genes—that determines what our body looks like
and, to a certain extent, how we behave. Our genes are a
mixture of each of our parents' genes. This is why we often

look like them and have the same traits. If your parents both have bright-red hair, then you are likely to have it too. And if they are both talented at sports, then you might be too.

He was born to be a goalkeeper!

2. NURTURE

The environment that you are born into and the way you are brought up also play a big part in who you are. If you play sports from an early age and put in hours and hours of practice, you have a better chance of making it as a professional.

So it is a combination of nature and nurture that makes us the people we are.

KEEP IT IN THE FAMILY

If one (or both) of your parents is a soccer player, you will have both nature and nurture in your favor: sporty genes and a home environment where soccer is appreciated. Several children of professional soccer players have become professionals too. But these soccer families are very rare. Christian Pulisic's father, Mark, was a professional player, although he never played for the U.S. men's national team. There are only a handful of examples of parent-child combinations in which both played international soccer.

PLAYER	DAD
Ty Keough	Harry Keogh
Alain Maca	Joe Maca
Taylor Twellman	Tim Twellman

There are other cases of soccer families involving siblings or married couples—whose children might grow to be talented players themselves!

PLAYER	RELATIVE
Archie Stark	Tommy Stark (brother)
Angelo DiBernardo	Paul DiBernardo (brother)
Claudio Reyna	Danielle Egan (wife)
Sydney Leroux	Dom Dwyer (husband)

So don't be put off your soccer dreams if neither your parents nor family are professional athletes. Hardly anyone else's are either.

HOW MUCH PRACTICE, MOM?

Whatever help you get from your family, continual practice is crucial to becoming an amazing soccer player. The more you practice, the better you will be, but how much is enough? Some people say that if you spend ten thousand hours practicing anything, you will become an expert at it. That's a long time. If you spent twelve hours a day, every day, practicing free kicks, you would reach ten thousand hours only after two years and three months of doing nothing else. You would have no friends and a very boring life, but you would be great at free kicks.

Here are some other jobs that the ten-thousand-hour rule could apply to:

Finally, I've reached 10,000 hours.

Pianist

Ice-skater

LOOT

Master criminal

HAPPY BIRTHDAYS, UNHAPPY BIRTHDAYS

Belgian midfielder Eden Hazard had the ideal childhood for becoming a soccer player. Both nature and nurture were on his side. His dad, Thierry, and his mom, Carine, were both soccer players. And behind his backyard in Belgium was a field where he practiced his tricks day after day. (But who knows if it was for ten thousand hours?) Hazard had one other factor that helped his aim of becoming a soccer player. He was born on January 7.

This date makes a difference, because you have more chance of succeeding as a young player if you are born earlier in the year and are one of the oldest on your team. In Belgium, where Hazard was born, the age cutoff is January 1. This means that the oldest players in the year are born in January and the youngest in December. For a long time, the United States was different, with a cutoff of September 1 for most state youth leagues, so the oldest players were born in September and the youngest in August. But recently the leagues switched to a January 1 cutoff to align with European youth soccer.

In leagues, older children are often bigger, faster, and stronger than their younger teammates, since they have had a few extra months to grow. And if you are bigger, faster, and stronger, you are likely to get picked to play more often, which in turn will help you improve, so you have more chances of getting picked for a high-school or club team, and then a chance to play professionally or for the Olympic or national teams.

This phenomenon helps explain this curious fact: children who are born just after the cutoff date for league soccer dominate the club teams. There are three times as many January-born kids on the under-sixteen club teams than there are December-born kids. Nick Levett, the English Football Association's former development manager, says of this phenomenon in his own country: "The simple fact is that adults have voted [later-born kids] out of the game because of our desire to pick bigger, stronger, faster players."

But it is not all good news for those who are born early in

PLAYERS BORN ON JANUARY 1
Roberto Rivellino (Brazil)
Davor Šuker (Croatia)
Lilian Thuram (France)
Jack Wilshere (England)
Steven Davis (N. Ireland)

the year. Yes, they are more likely to become professional soccer players at a young age—but they could also be more likely to get injured and end their careers earlier.

It's a bit like the fable of the hare and the tortoise. The hare sprints into an early lead, but it is the plodding tortoise that gets there in the end. Children who are born later in the year tend to join teams later but often have the longest careers.

TEAM AGES

Soccer leagues are only beginning to understand how important it is to make sure that *all* children have a chance to make it when they are still school age, not just the ones born soon after the cutoff. Often players who are born late in the year slip through the net, a shame for them and soccer.

The Netherlands team Ajax has introduced a new system to tackle this problem. Their youth league doesn't split children into under-eights, under-nines, and under-tens. Instead it has three broader age groups: six to eleven, twelve to fifteen, and sixteen to nineteen. These categories mean that even those born at the beginning of the school year will sometimes be playing with older players. Each player will have a different experience: sometimes being the oldest in the age category and sometimes being the youngest. It is hoped that this will eliminate the relative age effect.

Professional teams have also started to take note and now organize tournaments with young players picked not based on their age but according to their physical maturity. And that's what we believe here at Soccer School. Age and size should make no difference as to how you do anything. If you're good, you're good!

GREVILLE AND NEVILLE

☆ STAR STUDENT

"Mamma Mia!"

☆☆☆ STAR STUDENT stats

Siblings: 17
Age difference: 120 seconds
Freckle count (Greville): 300
Freckle count (Neville): 301
Birthplace: Twin Falls, Idaho
Support: Motherwell (Scotland)
Fave player: Ashley Young
Trick: Never forget a birthday

PHYS. ED. QUIZ

1. **France midfielder Paul Pogba's older twin brothers, Florentin and Mathias, play for which national team?**

a) France
b) Guinea
c) Ivory Coast
d) Australia

2. **To play the game Happy Families, you need:**

a) A special pack of cards
b) A great-grandmother
c) A soccer ball
d) An open space

3. **What was unusual about the substitution of Arnór Guðjohnsen when Iceland played Estonia in 1996?**

a) His wife was having a baby in the stands.
b) His son Eiður replaced him.
c) He got married on the field before the game.
d) His sister was the assistant coach.

4. **What was special about Toni Vidigal, Luís Vidigal, and Beto Vidigal, who played midfield for the Portuguese team O Elvas CAD in 1993?**

a) They had the same last name but were not related.
b) They were cousins and their uncle Victor was the coach.
c) They were brothers.
d) In the same season, three Vidigals also played for the local women's team, Elvenses.

5. **Alex is looking at a picture of a man and states, "Brothers and sisters have I none, but that man's father is my father's son." Who is the man in the picture?**

a) Alex's son
b) Alex
c) Alex's father
d) Ben

Soccer as we know it now is only about 150 years old, which, for historians, makes it a recent invention. But for the thousands of years before soccer, people across the world played other types of ball games.

Very recent.

In this lesson, we are going to go back in time to look at three of these ancient sports. One is from China, one is from Japan, and the other is from Central America. We'll see how all these games contain elements of what soccer is today.

We're not, however, going to encourage anyone to play these sports here at Soccer School. The rules would require us to smear the losing team with white powder, whip them in public, or chop their heads off. The classroom would get very messy!

CUJU

Where played: China, Korea, Vietnam

When: From about 200 BCE to 1400 CE

The ball: Spherical. Originally it was stitched leather stuffed with fur or feathers, but in later years, it was filled with air, a bit like balls today.

The goal: Sometimes crescent-shaped, sometimes a sheet with a hole in it suspended from two bamboo posts.

The rules: Two teams of up to sixteen players faced each other on a field with goals at each end. Players were not allowed to use their hands.

Uniform: Long robes.

Who played: At first, only soldiers in the army who spent a lot of time on horses played *cuju*, in order to get the blood circulating in their legs. Later the game spread to civilians and royalty; women were allowed to play. Over time, the best players were able to make a living as *cuju* professionals in organized leagues.

When played: At royal feasts and diplomatic events.

Winners' prize: Silver bowls or nice fabric.

Losers' prize: Their faces smeared with white powder and a public whipping.

Famous players: Emperor Wu of Han.

Spin-offs: A type of *cuju* with no goals, where two teams had to pass the ball to each other and were penalized for making mistakes, was also popular. Players were allowed to use any part of their body to pass the ball except their hands.

How is *cuju* similar to soccer? It was an organized game with two teams using a spherical ball, in which the aim was to score more goals than your opponent. It was very popular, with professional leagues and famous players.

What else was going on at the time? *Cuju* emerged at the same time that China changed from being a collection of warring states to a single empire, ruled by an emperor. In order to protect this new empire from tribes to the north, the Chinese started to build a wall that got so big and long, it's now known as the Great Wall of China.

Under the rule of *cuju*-playing Emperor Wu of Han, who lived between 156 and 87 BCE, China expanded to include parts of Korea and Vietnam.

The ancient Chinese invented many things, such as paper, steel, porcelain, and gunpowder. By the time of *cuju*'s demise, China was the most advanced civilization in the world.

KEMARI

Where played: Japan
When: 600 to 1900 CE
The ball: Hollow, spherical, and made from deerskin.

The field: A square bounded by four trees, one at each corner. For this reason, the game was also known as "Standing Among the Trees." The trees were usually a pine, a cherry, a willow, and a maple.

The aim: *Kemari* was just like juggling a soccer ball as a group. The players kicked the ball in the air as many times as they could without letting it touch the ground, while passing it among themselves.

The rules: Players were allowed to use their upper bodies to knock the ball down to their feet or legs. They could also bounce the ball off the trees.

Uniform: Formal Japanese clothing with very large sleeves, and a rimless hat. Socks were color-coded according to rank and skill.

Who played: Warriors and royals.

Language: When a player kicked a ball to himself, he shouted "Ari," "Ya," or "Oh," which are the names of gods who were believed to live in the trees.

Positions: Between six and eight people played the game, standing in a circle. The best four players were each in front of one of the trees.

The game: The players walked onto the field in order of rank, with the highest coming on first. All players had a practice kick to get used to the ball. The game started when the player of the highest rank kicked off. The game ended when the same player kicked the ball high and caught it in his robes.

Length of a game: Usually about fifteen minutes, although an old text says that an emperor and his *kemari* team once kept the ball in the air for more than one thousand kicks.

Still around today? Yes. A few Japanese people have preserved the tradition. Former U.S. president George H. W. Bush played *kemari* on an official visit to Japan in 1992.

How is *kemari* similar to soccer? *Kemari* was a kicking game using a spherical ball that is almost identical to skills-training games that soccer players play today.

What else was going on at the time? From around 1100 until 1600, Japan was a country dominated by warriors called samurai. These fierce fighters had distinctive armor and were famous for their long, curved swords, their self-discipline, and their code of honor. Gradually samurai principles of loyalty and duty became part of Japanese culture generally.

In the 1630s, Japan's military leader banned all foreigners from entering the country and all Japanese people from leaving it. For the next two hundred years, Japan was almost totally disconnected from the rest of the world. During this period, they kept on playing *kemari*. Sushi—blocks of rice with raw fish on top—was invented, and activities such as puppet theater and writing haiku also flourished around this time.

A haiku is a poem written in three lines, with five syllables in the first and last lines and seven in the middle line. Usually a haiku makes an observation about life or nature. Here are two we've written on our favorite subject:

Soccer Haiku

Everything is fun
At the Soccer School of joy
Then the whistle blows

No one loves soccer
More than Alex and Ben do
Except maybe you

PITZ

Where played: Central America (the area including Mexico, Guatemala, Belize, Honduras, Nicaragua, El Salvador, and Costa Rica)

When: 1500 BCE to 1500 CE

Who played: The Olmecs, the Maya, and the Aztecs, among others.

The ball: Bouncy! The Central Americans were the first people to discover how to make rubber,

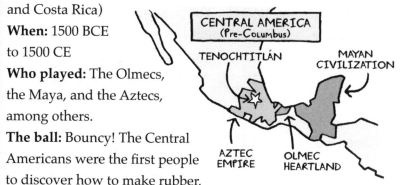

CENTRAL AMERICA
(Pre-Columbus)

TENOCHTITLÁN

MAYAN CIVILIZATION

AZTEC EMPIRE

OLMEC HEARTLAND

which comes from latex—a milky substance found in a tree. The balls made for *pitz* were solid rubber and probably a bit bigger and heavier than a basketball.

The field: Narrower than a soccer field, and sometimes shaped like a capital I. There were usually sloping stone walls on the left and right sides of the field. Archaeologists, people who study the remains of civilizations, have discovered more than 1,500 *pitz* fields. The field sizes vary from smaller than a tennis court to about the size of a full-length soccer field.

The goals: Most of the fields didn't have goals, but toward the end of the Mayan period, people started to hang a stone ring high up on each of the two side walls. The idea seems to have been to get the ball through the ring, although this was probably quite difficult to do.

The rules: No one knows the rules anymore; it's probable that over three thousand years, they changed a lot. The most likely theory is that two teams would face each other and bounce the ball between them using only their hips.

Uniform: Pictures and sculptures from the era show that the basic uniform consisted of a loincloth and a hip guard. But there were many accessories: helmets, headdresses, chest protectors, shin pads, and gloves.

Dangers: The ball was very heavy, and historians believe that players got bruised a lot. Some players may have died when the ball hit them in the head or stomach.

Purpose: The game was an important religious ritual and also sometimes used as a way of settling disputes.

Religious significance? The sacred book of the Maya is called the Popol Vuh. It had the same function as the Bible does for Christians or the Koran does for Muslims, in that it provided stories about the creation of the world. The central story is based around a game of *pitz*. The two heroes are the twins Hunahpú and Xbalanqué. The lords of the underworld—they're the equivalent of the devil—challenged the twins to a ball game. After many hair-raising escapades in the underworld, including the time that Hunahpú's head was chopped off by a bat and used as the ball (a turtle made him a new one), eventually Hunahpú and Xbalanqué defeated the evil empire. When they reentered the real world, the twins rose high into the sky and became the sun and the moon.

Winners' prize: Treated to a feast.

Losers' prize: Their heads were chopped off. Some historians say that their skulls were then used as the basis of a new ball.

Still around today? Yes. The game of *ulama*, which is descended from *pitz*, is still played in a few places in Mexico.

How is *pitz* similar to soccer? *Pitz* was a ball game between two teams in which you were not allowed to use your hands. It was hugely popular and culturally important. Large stadiums were built to play and watch it.

What else was going on at the time? Chocolate! The cocoa bean, which is the main ingredient in chocolate, is native to the Americas and was made into a drink enjoyed all over Central America. It tasted very different from the chocolate we eat now because the Maya and the Aztecs didn't have sugar. Instead, they mixed ground cocoa beans with water, chili peppers, and cornmeal. Wow!

MAYA GOLDBERG

STAR
☆ STUDENT

66 Watch your head! 99

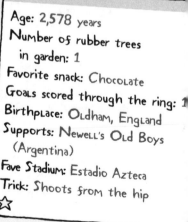

☆ STAR
☆ STUDENT stats

Age: 2,578 years
Number of rubber trees
  in garden: 1
Favorite snack: Chocolate
Goals scored through the ring: 1
Birthplace: Oldham, England
Supports: Newell's Old Boys
  (Argentina)
Fave Stadium: Estadio Azteca
Trick: Shoots from the hip
☆

HISTORY QUIZ

1. What did the ancient Chinese build along their northern border that is thousands of miles long?

a) A running track
b) A wall
c) A zip wire
d) A football field

2. Which of these countries is situated where the ancient Mayan civilization was centered?

a) Greenland
b) Great Britain
c) Guatemala
d) Japan

3. The samurai sword was special in what way?

a) It was straight.
b) It had two blades.
c) It had a long grip for both hands.
d) It was made of gold.

4. Which of the following did the Chinese NOT invent?

a) Toothpaste
b) Printing
c) Silk
d) The compass

5. The Olmecs were the first major civilization in Central America. What does their name mean?

a) Rubber people
b) Fierce people
c) Ball people
d) Chosen people

Ball person →

S coring a penalty kick should be easy. You place the ball on the white spot a few yards in front of the goal and then kick it, with only the goalkeeper standing in your way.

But penalties are not that easy.

Some of the best players in the world, including Alex's soccer pal Pelé, have missed important penalty kicks. Argentinian midfielder Diego Maradona, one of soccer's best-ever players, once missed five in a row!

Luckily we have a world expert on penalty kicks here at Soccer School. Ben spent two years studying everything there is to know about penalty kicks and even wrote a great book on them. In this lesson, he will reveal his five best tips for scoring the perfect penalty.

It's good that we're in the classroom and not out on the field, because the overwhelming message is that when it comes to penalty kicks, the most important part of your body is not your foot, but your brain.

ON THE SPOT
Penalty kicks happen when:
1. The referee believes a foul or a handball has taken place in the penalty area.
2. A knockout game ends with the score tied after extra time. Then there is a penalty shoot-out— each team takes five penalty kicks, and whoever scores the most wins.

BEN'S TIPS FOR THE PERFECT PENALTY KICK

Imagine you are about to take a penalty kick in front of a stadium packed full of fans. Follow these terrific tips from Ben and learn how to be at the top of your mental game.

BEN'S TIP No. 1
BE POSITIVE

Read this carefully: I want you to clear your mind of all thoughts about elephants.

Absolutely do NOT think about elephants.

Especially a pink elephant in a tutu.

Are we ready? I bet you are thinking about a pink elephant in a tutu.

You are having these thoughts because it is impossible for humans to *not* think about something that has been suggested to them. We can't do it!

In the same way, if you are about to take a penalty, you should not say to yourself, "I must not miss, I must not miss." Because thinking about NOT missing is the same as thinking about missing.

And you don't want to be thinking about missing, because then you will be more likely to miss. When you take a penalty, you want to be thinking about scoring.

In order not to fill your mind with thoughts about missing, **focus** hard on what you are doing—for example, counting the steps in your run-up. And think, "I will score."

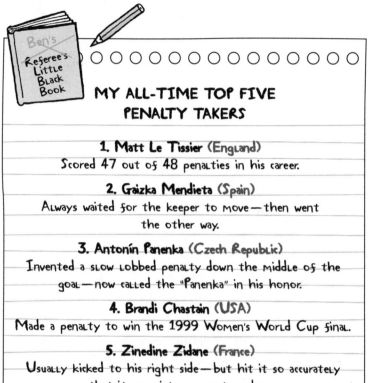

MY ALL-TIME TOP FIVE PENALTY TAKERS

1. Matt Le Tissier (England)
Scored 47 out of 48 penalties in his career.

2. Gaizka Mendieta (Spain)
Always waited for the keeper to move—then went the other way.

3. Antonín Panenka (Czech Republic)
Invented a slow lobbed penalty down the middle of the goal—now called the "Panenka" in his honor.

4. Brandi Chastain (USA)
Made a penalty to win the 1999 Women's World Cup final.

5. Zinedine Zidane (France)
Usually kicked to his right side—but hit it so accurately that it was virtually unstoppable.

BEN'S TIP No. 2
TAKE YOUR TIME

The English national team has two world records when it comes to penalties:

1. England misses more penalties in shoot-outs than any other national team.
2. Once the ref blows the whistle, England players take their penalties quicker on average than any other country.

Do you think these two records are related? Of course they are! Rushing can lead to mistakes, in life and in soccer.

So my advice is this: Once the ref blows the whistle, be calm. **Don't rush. Take an extra breath. Compose yourself.** Make sure you are ready. And then take the penalty.

HUG YOUR TEAMMATES (EVEN IF THEY MISS)

Team spirit is really important for staying positive. You need to feel it in the good times and the bad. In fact, you need it more when things get bad.

So if players miss penalties, don't get angry with them. Walk up to them, **give them a hug,** and say nice things to them.

Trust me: teams that celebrate goals and hug players who miss in penalty shoot-outs are more likely to win the penalty shoot-outs.

If players know that they will still be loved by their team even if they miss, they become less scared of missing and therefore more likely to score.

He missed!

BEN'S TIP No. 4
KEEP EYE CONTACT WITH THE KEEPER

Once the ball is on the penalty spot, you need to mark out your run-up. You have two choices. Either you can walk backward, while always keeping an eye on the goal and the goalkeeper, or you can walk with your back to the keeper before turning around to face the ball.

Most England players walk with their back to the keeper, thus avoiding eye contact with him. And we know that lots of England players miss!

Some psychologists think that avoiding eye contact shows fear and gives the goalkeeper an advantage. Instead, it's better to face the challenge head-on. **Keep eye contact.** Let your opponent think you are confident. That will make *them* start worrying!

BEN'S TIP No. 5
PRACTICE WITH PURPOSE

When England lost a penalty shoot-out to Italy in Euro 2012, England coach Roy Hodgson said that practicing penalties before the game had been no help: "You can't reproduce the pressure. You can't reproduce the nervous tension." Previous England coaches have said something very similar.

They are right. You can't.

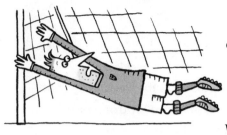

But the same is true of most sports: you can never copy the exact conditions for a tennis player serving to win Wimbledon, or a golfer putting to win the Ryder Cup, or a cyclist scaling a hill climb at the Tour de France. But those athletes still practice, don't they?

In fact, a tennis player, a golfer, and a cyclist all told me the same thing: they practice with purpose. That means they pretend the situation is exactly the same, even if it isn't. They try to copy the conditions as much as possible. Cyclists don't practice hill climbs on flat roads, do they? No. They find a hill and climb it! And they make it competitive, with prizes for winning and forfeits for losing.

That's how players can practice for penalties—with purpose. So that means taking penalties at the end of a game when you're tired. It means practicing the long walk from the center circle to the penalty spot in a shoot-out. It means waiting for the referee to blow the whistle and imagining the world is watching. **Preparation for anything will increase your chances of success.** Penalties are no different!

In fact, we think you can handle tricky situations in life in the same way you handle penalties.

Anytime you face a tough challenge, use this handy summary of Ben's five tips to help you.

They work from the penalty spot on the field, so why not off the field too?

1. Focus.
2. Don't rush.
3. Be supportive.
4. Look the challenge in the eye.
5. Be prepared.

MY ALL-TIME TOP FIVE PENALTY SHOOT-OUTS

West Germany 5, France 4 (1982 World Cup semifinal)
The first World Cup shoot-out, and the first on live TV

Brazil 3, Italy 2 (1994 World Cup final)
The world's best player at the time, Roberto Baggio, missed the final penalty and Italy lost.

KK Palace 17, Civics 16 (2005 Namibian Cup final)
It took a world-record 48 kicks for this shoot-out to end.

Liverpool 3, AC Milan 2 (2005 Champions League final)
The Reds' keeper Jerzy Dudek waved his arms to put off kickers.

Netherlands U21 13, England U21 12
(2007 European Under-21 Championship semifinal)
Netherlands' body-language expert told players to give positive signals.

TWELVE YARDS

The penalty spot is twelve yards, or about eleven meters, from the goal.

In German, the word for penalty kick is "elfmeter," which translates as "eleven meters,, since *elf* is the German word for eleven. So *elfmeter* has nothing to do with measuring Santa's little helpers!

STAR STUDENT

BRIAN POWER

"Heads up!"

STAR STUDENT stats

Positive thoughts per game: 86
Steps in run-up: 11
Length of wait before taking penalty: 5.6 seconds
Average penalty speed: 58 mph/ 93 kmh
Birthplace: Braintree, Massachusetts
Supports: Penafiel (Portugal)
Fave player: Tom Cleverley
Trick: Impossible to tell which way he will shoot

PSYCHOLOGY QUIZ

1. **What is a penalty kick that is slowly chipped down the middle of the goal called?**

a) Zidane

b) Panenka

c) Unlucky

d) Le Tissier

2. **What happens if the scores are even in a penalty shoot-out after both teams have taken five penalties?**

a) The coaches take penalties.

b) They keep going until one team misses and the other scores.

c) The captains play rock-paper-scissors.

d) They flip a coin.

3. **What was special about Martin Palermo's performance for Argentina in a 1999 Copa América game against Colombia?**

a) He scored three penalties.

b) He missed three penalties.

c) He scored a penalty and saved a penalty.

d) He broke the crossbar with a penalty.

4. **What did French midfielder Zinedine Zidane do before scoring a penalty against England at the 2004 European Championship?**

a) He kissed the referee.

b) He sang the French national anthem, "La Marseillaise."

c) He barfed on the edge of the penalty area.

d) He shook the hands of all his teammates for luck.

5. **Why is Alex Molodetsky famous in the world of penalties?**

a) He trained elephants to score penalties.

b) He once scored a penalty with his head.

c) He could save penalties blindfolded.

d) He invented a ball that veers into the goal even if it's aimed off target.

In the last lesson, we forgot to mention another essential element in penalty-taking. Indeed, this element is essential for all parts of the game. If you want to play well, you need a good pair of shoes.

Imagine playing in shoes that went over your ankles. They would be heavier than the shoes you play in today. You would run more slowly and use up more energy. Not great!

Yet that is what soccer shoes were like up until the 1950s.

Shoemakers today put a lot of thought into the design of soccer shoes and the materials they use to make them. In this lesson, we are going to see how the design of shoes has changed over time. But first, let's see just what a difference the right shoes can make to a game.

ALL YOU CAN CLEAT

Hungary was a big favorite to win the 1954 World Cup final against West Germany in Bern, Switzerland. But the Mighty Magyars lost 3–2, handing the Germans their first World Cup trophy. Many commentators said the Germans' victory was due to their shoes, which had screw-in cleats. It rained heavily, and the field was muddy: the Germans

were able to screw in larger cleats to their regular shoes, giving them an advantage on the slippy turf. After that game, everyone in soccer realized just how important it is to have the right shoes.

A HIS-TOE-RY OF SOCCER FOOTWEAR

1500s

King Henry VIII owned one of the earliest pairs of shoes specifically made for playing soccer. We know he had a pair because they were listed in a palace document as having been made by his personal shoemaker, Cornelius Johnson, in 1526. Historians think the shoes were

ankle-high, made from strong leather, and heavier than normal shoes. In the Tudor period, soccer wasn't the game we play today but a kind of organized brawl that often led to riots. Off the field, Henry VIII could be ruthless: he had six wives and chopped the heads off two of them. So pity anyone who got in his way during a game.

1850-1900

The first shoes designed solely for modern soccer were made from thick leather and had leather cleats to grip the turf. They were heavy and doubled in weight when wet.

1900-1950

Famous cleat producers, such as Gola in the U.K. and Hummel in Germany, opened for business. One big German company, the Dassler Brothers Shoe Factory, introduced replaceable cleats that could be changed depending on the weather. Later the company split into two.

1950s

Brazilian designers removed the ankle part of the soccer shoe. English forward Stanley Matthews saw Brazil play in the 1950 World Cup and bought a pair of their shoes. He returned home and asked the Heckmondwike Boot and Shoe Works to copy them. The lower-cut design was lighter, allowing players to run faster.

1960-1970

Leather was replaced by lighter materials such as rubber. In 1970, English midfielder Alan Ball became the first player to wear white shoes. He was paid £2,000 by Hummel to do so. But Hummel didn't have a pair that fit, so the marketing director painted Ball's Adidas shoes white and then added chevrons to make them look like Hummels.

1980s

English team Liverpool's ex-midfielder Craig Johnston wanted to help kids he was coaching control the ball better, so he designed a new shoe, the Adidas Predator, which had rubber fins. The Predator is still worn today, and other shoe designers have followed his lead.

2000-PRESENT

In recent years, new technology has inspired lots of weird and wacky shoes. These include shoes without laces and shoes made using sharkskin leather, with holes in the soles like gills.

I LOVE MY sharkskin shoes!

MATERIAL WORLD

Soccer shoes need to be many things. They need to be comfy so players enjoy wearing them. They need to be tough so the feet are protected. They need to be hard-wearing so they don't fall apart in the middle of a game, and they need to be light so they don't weigh players down. These factors decide the many different materials that go into the modern shoe.

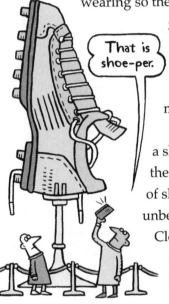

That is shoe-per.

The cleats are the hardest part of a shoe. The cleat's job is to penetrate the ground so that you can grip instead of slipping. The material must be unbendable, unbreakable, and tough. Cleats are usually made from a light metal such as **aluminum**, or a hard **plastic**, or a mixture of both.

The sole of a shoe has to be stiff enough to keep the cleats in place, flexible enough so that it doesn't shatter when you run, and hard enough to protect the foot. The most suitable material is a light plastic, but one that is more flexible than the hard plastic used for cleats. Some shoes use a plastic that bends in only one direction, since the extra stiffness that you get from it not bending in the other direction can increase the power of a kick.

The "upper" of the shoe covers the sides and top of your foot. It needs to be flexible so you can control the ball and so it's comfy when you run. The material also has to be

tough so you are
protected if you
are stepped on,
and so it doesn't
get damaged when
you kick the ball. **Leather** is
best for this job, as it is very
hard-wearing and performs well in all temperatures
and weather conditions. Scientists have invented many
amazing materials, but when it comes to shoes, nothing is
as versatile as the skin of a cow.

Modern shoes also have plastic ridges and skins on the
upper that create texture to help you control the ball.

SHOE DESIGN TODAY

Tongue below laces creates
POWER SHOOTING

Textured fins and
panels improve
CONTROL and
PASSING

Solid grip for
high-speed DRIBBLING

Extra fabric for
CURLING
FREE KICKS

HAPPY FEET

The best players in the world don't have to go shopping for soccer shoes: shoemakers give them pairs for free.

When you play soccer every day, your feet develop extra muscle in the toes. In order to protect this muscle and not be too tight, professional players' shoes sometimes have more padding around the toes. And what's more, the shoemakers take a mold of each

MUSCLY TOE

player's feet and use it to make shoes that will fit perfectly, like a second skin. Argentinian forward Lionel Messi says he likes his shoes to "feel more like slippers than shoes." Maybe he should wear a bathrobe too!

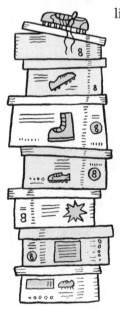

Most professionals rotate four or five pairs of shoes over a season; like your favorite clothes, they become more comfortable the more you wear them. But everyone is different: Dutch winger Memphis Depay told us he likes to wear his shoes fresh out of the box for big games.

CUSTOMIZE MY CLEATS

Players often like to personalize the design of their shoes with words or images:

PLAYER	SHOEMAKER	PERSONALIZATION
Pierre-Emerick Aubameyang	Nike	Encrusted with 4,000 Swarovski crystals and his initials, PEA
Lionel Messi	Adidas	Sons' names and Argentina flag
Mario Balotelli	Puma	Fake Mohawk hairstyle on the heel
Neymar	Nike	"Courage" and "joy" on side, NJR11 on the heel
Memphis Depay	Under Armour	"Memphis" signature on the heel

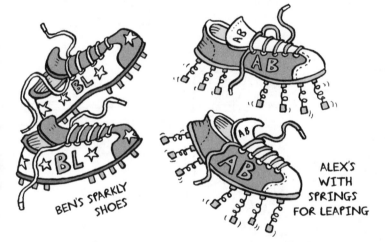

BEN'S SPARKLY SHOES

ALEX'S WITH SPRINGS FOR LEAPING

DON'T TREAD ON MY TOES

Not all players like to wear shoes. India was invited to play in the 1950 World Cup but did not show up after the organizers, FIFA, said that all players had to wear shoes. Some of the players on India's team had played in the 1948 Olympics wearing only bandages on their feet, as they found it more comfortable (and lighter).

FAMILY FEUD

Adidas and Puma are two of the biggest sports brands, but did you know they were founded by two brothers who hated each other? Adi and Rudolf Dassler started the Dassler Brothers Shoe Factory in the 1920s. But the brothers had a falling out, and in 1948 Adi established Adidas and Rudolf set up a company that became Puma. The two factories were in the same town in Germany, on opposite sides of the river. The brothers never made up.

"SPEEDY" STEVIE FINS

STAR STUDENT

66 Eat my cleats! 99

STAR STUDENT stats

Swerve factor: 180 degrees
Top speed: 100 mph/160 kmh
Soccer shoes: 100 pairs
Dress shoes: 1 pair
Birthplace: Shubert, Nebraska
Supports: Boston Red Sox
Fave player: Wilfried Bony
Trick: Ball sticks to his shoes

DESIGN TECHNOLOGY QUIZ

1. What is the name of the top part of a soccer shoe?

a) The downer
b) The middler
c) The upper
d) The topper

2. Which of these is a desirable property of the sole of a soccer shoe?

a) Elastic
b) Porous
c) Aromatic
d) Rigid

3. Why do referees check players' cleats before they come on the field?

a) To make sure they don't have chewing gum on their soles
b) To ensure the cleats are not sharp or dangerous to opponents
c) To check that both shoes have the same number of cleats
d) It's a tradition dating back to horse-drawn carts, when drivers used to check horses' hooves.

4. What would be the most sensible material for shoelaces from the ones below?

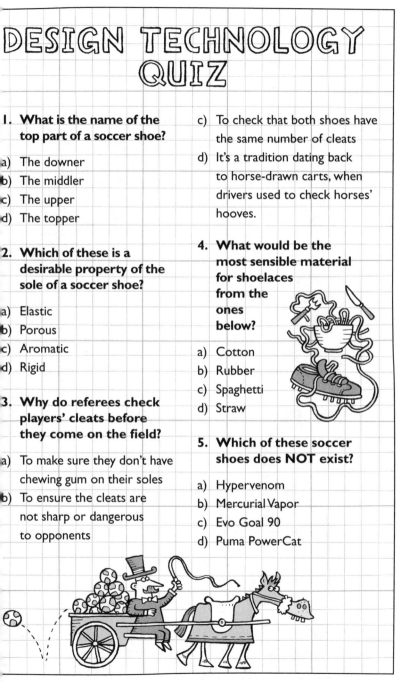

a) Cotton
b) Rubber
c) Spaghetti
d) Straw

5. Which of these soccer shoes does NOT exist?

a) Hypervenom
b) Mercurial Vapor
c) Evo Goal 90
d) Puma PowerCat

For this lesson, we're going to fly down to Brazil, the most successful country in international soccer. Brazil has won the World Cup more times than anyone else: in 1958, 1962, 1970, 1994, and 2002.

Brazil has also produced more great players than any other nation and continues to have more professional players on teams around the world than anyone else.

So how come the Brazilians are so good? What have they got that no one else has? Alex used to live in Rio de Janeiro, and this is what he found out.

BIG IS BEAUTIFUL

Brazil is the largest country in South America. It's huge—bigger even than the continental United States. It is also the world's fifth most populous country, with more than 210 million people. So that's one reason there are lots of Brazilian soccer players: there are lots of Brazilians.

If you look at how many people live in each country in the world, you can see that Brazil is in the top five:

COUNTRY	POPULATION	% OF WORLD POPULATION
China	1.4 billion	19%
India	1.3 billion	18%
USA	326 million	4%
Indonesia	265 million	4%
Brazil	210 million	3%

TROPICAL TURF TROUBLES

Brazil also has lots of animals, including armadillos, monkeys, sloths, and vampire bats. In fact, it has more species of animals than any other country. This variety is called **biodiversity** and is due to Brazil being a tropical country with many different habitats, such as rain forest, desert, savanna, and swamps. The climate is nearly always hot, and the weather alternates between blistering sun and torrential rainstorms.

When it comes to soccer, Brazilians tend to be very skillful players. They are known for their ball control and their repertoire of tricks. Believe it or not, the extreme weather plays an important part in this.

Thunderous downpours and scorching heat are great for the plants that live in the rain forest—but terrible for grass.

In Brazil, it is almost impossible to maintain a grass lawn . . . or a soccer field. In fact, the country has almost NO grass soccer fields. Schools don't have grass fields for children to practice on, and there are hardly any parks. The few grass fields that exist in Brazil are mostly in stadiums, where gardeners have to tend them every day.

You might think that because almost no young Brazilians learn to play on grass, they would be WORSE, not better, players, but as we will see, the opposite is the case.

MEGACITIES

Most Brazilians live in towns and cities. Brazil's cities have grown so fast in recent decades that many of them have populations of several million. The biggest city, São Paulo, is home to almost as many people as the whole of Australia.

These megacities are crammed full, with few large open spaces for people to run around in (apart from the beach, if the city has one). In the poorest parts of these cities, there are almost no roads: simple brick homes are built on top of one another with only tiny pathways between them. There is hardly any space to swing a cat, let alone kick a ball. But the Brazilians use this to their advantage too.

POPULATION OF BIGGEST CITIES

| Brasília (the capital) 4 million | Porto Alegre 4 million | Belo Horizonte 5 million | Rio de Janeiro 12 million | São Paulo 20 million |

THE ADVANTAGES OF DISADVANTAGES

With no grass fields and little space in cities to play soccer, instead people learn the game on patches of dirt and on the street.

If you are playing on gnarled, knobbly terrain where the ball will bounce in unpredictable directions, you will develop really fast reactions and good technique.

ROUGH TERRAIN

If you are playing on concrete, where you can't fall without hurting yourself, you will develop amazing control and balance. If you are playing soccer in tiny spaces, you will develop excellent ball skills.

CONCRETE

In other words, one of the reasons Brazil's soccer players are so good is that the geography—that's the climate and the cities—provides so many obstacles to playing.

TINY SPACE

A FIELD WITH A DIFFERENCE

There are two other places where the Brazilians find space to play soccer, and they are also important:

1. INDOORS

Because of the lack of outdoor fields, many young Brazilians learn to play soccer indoors on a hard court floor. The indoor game is called *futsal*. It is five-a-side soccer played on a field roughly the size of a basketball court and using a smaller, heavier ball.

Because the *futsal* ball does not bounce very well, it requires much more technique to master. *Futsal* players have less space to move around in than soccer players on a full-size field, which means that *futsal* players have to be very quick, with better close-ball control and no fear of dribbling. The result is that if you play *futsal*, you become a fast and fearless player.

Futsal was invented in Uruguay, Brazil's neighbor, but the game became more popular in Brazil than anywhere else. In fact, more Brazilians play *futsal* than play soccer.

Brazil even has a professional *futsal* league. Many of the country's best soccer players started out playing *futsal*. Now we know why they are so good!

STAR FUTSALLERS

Marta
Neymar
Pelé
Ronaldinho
Zico

2. THE BEACH

Brazil has about five thousand miles of coastline, and beaches cover much of it. There are beaches in many of Brazil's major cities—such as Rio de Janeiro, Santos, Salvador, and Recife—and soccer gets played on them.

Beach soccer is much harder to play than normal soccer because you need more energy to run on sand. Since the ball hardly bounces, you have to be much more accurate with passes and also use lots of different parts of your body to control the ball. So if you play beach soccer, you will be very fit and have great technique.

DANCING OFF THE FIELD

In addition to the sun, the rain, the cities, the indoor courts, and the beaches, Brazilians have another big advantage when it comes to soccer: they love to dance. Brazil's national musical style is called samba. Samba is very fast, uplifting, and rhythmical and is usually played on percussion instruments such as small drums, shakers, and the tambourine. Samba also has its own special style of dancing, in which you tap your feet and wiggle your hips a lot. Children growing up in Brazil learn how to samba, so they learn to move their feet and shake their hips much better than children in other countries do. Wiggling your hips is very useful in soccer—for wiggling past defenders and twisting your body to strike the ball.

WHO NEEDS A BALL, ANYWAY?

Brazil has many families who are too poor to buy a soccer ball for their children to play with. Lots of people told Alex that it's common for children from these families to learn to play soccer using coconuts, oranges, and even eggs.

If you learn to play soccer with a coconut, you are going to get sore feet. If you learn with an orange, you are going to get sticky feet. And if you learn with an egg, someone is going to get splattered!

But there are advantages to using such unconventional (and tasty) objects as balls. It is much more difficult to play soccer with fruit than it is with a nice pumped-up ball, so children who learn with unusual objects are going to develop better ball skills. Imagine trying to do keepy-uppies with an egg! (We do not suggest you try this at home.)

You will need to have an almost insane level of control to kick and catch the egg without it breaking.

So when we look at Brazil, we can see that for aspiring soccer players, adversity breeds creativity. This means that the greater a challenge is, the more resourceful you need to be to overcome it. Young Brazilians are faced with many challenges when it comes to playing soccer, and as a result they develop amazing, world-beating skills.

In 1953, Brazil launched a competition to design the national team's uniform. The winning entry of a yellow jersey with green collar and cuffs—which is still worn today—was sent in by a teenager who had never designed a soccer uniform before!

STAR STUDENT

SMITHZINHO

66 God is Brazilian! 99

STAR STUDENT **stats**

Daily intake of coconuts: 5
Juggling record: 7,563
Number of "o"s in gooooooooooal: 10
Biodiversity of garden: 17 species of monkeys, 250 species of cockroaches, and 1 sloth
Birthplace: Copacabana
Team: Anyone but Argentina
Fave player: Rio Ferdinand
☆ Trick: Can dance around players

GEOGRAPHY QUIZ

1. What is the capital of Brazil?

a) Belo Horizonte
b) Brasília
c) Rio de Janeiro
d) São Paulo

2. The biggest team in São Paulo, Brazil's largest city, is named after which British team?

a) Corinthians
b) Wanderers
c) Spartans
d) Rangers

3. What is the name of the razor-toothed Amazon fish that likes to eat raw flesh and is strong enough to bite your finger off?

a) Anaconda
b) Caiman
c) South American Finger-Muncher
d) Piranha

4. What is the full name of FIFA Player of the Century Pelé?

a) Ronaldo de Assis Moreira
b) Mário Jorge Lobo Zagallo
c) Edson Arantes do Nascimento
d) Diego Armando Maradona Franco

5. Brazil's flag is a blue circle inside a yellow diamond on a green background. But what is in the blue circle?

a) 1 military cross
b) 5 soccer balls
c) 8 scorpions
d) 27 white stars

I n some ways, soccer players are like famous actors. People pay to see them perform live. You can watch them on prime-time television. They feature in ads and celebrity magazines. And, on the field, they also do a lot of acting.

In this lesson, we are going to look at the different ways soccer players act. There's both good and bad acting. Everyone loves the player or team who celebrates their goal with a jubilant piece of theater. On the other hand, fans and commentators criticize players who scream in pretend agony when they are not really hurt.

We'll see how soccer often involves acting without words and how, sometimes, the game is as dramatic as the plays of ancient Greece—although you don't need to wear a toga to enjoy this lesson.

THE GOAL-CELEBRATION OSCAR

First, let's look at some of the best celebrations in soccer. To do this, we have to go all the way to Iceland and a small team called Stjarnan. Thanks to some inspirational acting, for a brief moment this team was among the most famous in the world.

At the time, the team was playing in Iceland's first division. The players were friends as well as teammates, since they had all grown up in a small town called Garðabær and had played together for more than a dozen years. In Iceland, they were already famous for their funny goal celebrations—but then one elaborate performance caught the whole world's imagination.

In a game against rivals Fylkir, striker Halldór Orri Björnsson scored a match-winning penalty kick in the last minute. He ran to the edge of the area. He stretched out one arm as though he were casting a fishing rod. His teammate Jóhann Laxdal fell onto his side about six yards away. As Björnsson pretended to reel him in with his other hand, Laxdal flopped toward him, bouncing on his shoulder and hip like a fish out of water. Laxdal was apparently chosen for the role because in Icelandic, *laxdal* means "valley of the salmon."

There was more to come. Once Laxdal had flopped at the goal scorer's feet, four more teammates lifted him up and held him on his side, as though showing off their catch for a photo.

Another teammate, Baldvin Sturluson, got down on one knee and pretended to take a photo of the "salmon." The celebration was inevitably named "The Salmon." A video of it went viral and was watched by millions around the world, showing that soccer and drama make a great match.

Planning sequences of movement in this way is known as **choreography**. Stjarnan continued to celebrate their goals with choreographed theatrical flourishes. Here are some of their highlights. Action!

STJARNAN CELEBRATIONS

1. The Toilet—One player goes down on all fours, with two others behind him (they are the seat and flusher). The scorer sits on the back of the crouching player, pretends to read a newspaper, then stands up and pulls the hand of the flusher.

2. The Bicycle—Two players kneel on the ground with one lying in between them. The back player puts his hands on the front player's shoulders. The scorer jumps on the back player's shoulders and pedals, using the player on the floor.

3. The Diver—One player kneels on the ground, and the goal scorer dives off his back into an imaginary swimming pool and swims.

4. The Ballroom Dancers—The goal scorer grabs his nearest teammate and dances a waltz with him. Six other teammates pair up and do the same dance.

5. The Bobsled—Four players push an imaginary bar in the same direction, then sit in a line with legs outstretched. They lean left and then right as though in a bobsled.

ACTIONS SPEAK LOUDER THAN WORDS

There are other effective ways of acting on a field. When we watch soccer on TV or even in a stadium, we can't hear what the players are saying. But we know what they are thinking, because their bodies give it away. This is called **body language**. It's a way of communicating without words and is an important tool of an actor's trade.

The defender who puts the palms of his hands together and waves them in the direction of the referee? He wants justice. The striker who storms over and puts his nose right next to his opponent's nose? He is angry.

Sometimes our bodies respond in a natural way: we smile when we are happy; we grimace or cry out when we are hurt. But in a competitive environment like a soccer game, some players exaggerate their reactions to events. They are doing just what clowns in the circus do: overemphasizing their facial expressions and body gestures in order to communicate wordlessly. This is a type of acting called **mime**. Players use the techniques of mime so the other players, the referee, and the fans can understand their feelings on the field without them having to speak.

Here are some acting expressions that all players know (and also know how to exaggerate for maximum effect):

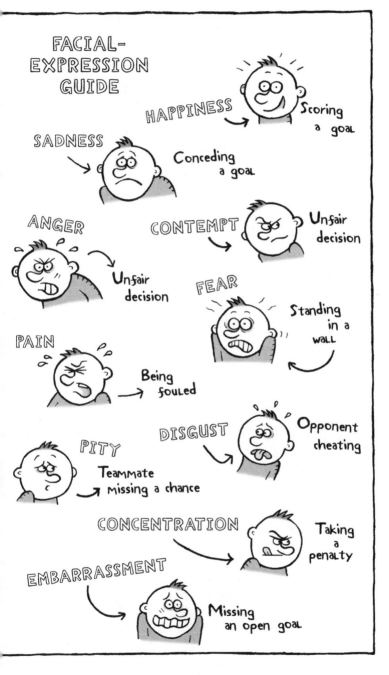

CROWD CHORUS

Soccer players may behave like actors, but watching a soccer game is different from watching a play or a film. When you are in the theater, cinema, or just watching TV at home, usually you want silence so you can hear what is going on.

Soccer is the opposite. You want to be noisy, because it means you are part of the action. If you're watching a game at a stadium and singing loudly enough, the players can hear you, which can inspire them to play well and can also distract their opponents.

Sometimes fans boo players if they used to play for their team in the past, or if they foul someone, or if they just have a bad haircut. These noises from the crowd—cheers for the heroes, boos for the villains—are a way of commenting on the main characters in the action.

This used to happen in the first plays, which were performed in ancient Greece nearly three thousand years ago. During a play, a group of actors called the **chorus** would stand near the stage and provide a commentary on the action.

They might sing a song to describe what a character is thinking or move the plot along by adding information. So think about it the next time you go to a game: your words can also become the story. That makes you an important part of the game.

DIVING COMPETITION

But perhaps the most common form of acting during a soccer game is when a player pretends to have been fouled so as to gain an advantage, either by winning a free kick or a penalty or by getting their opponent sent off.

This tactic is called diving. A player falls to the ground and writhes in agony. His teammates protest that the victim was pushed or kicked. Once the referee has made a decision, the player stands up, not looking so injured after all.

A survey of the first thirty-two games played at the 2014 World Cup revealed that of the 302 players who collapsed on the field during the tournament, only nine were injured. That's about 3 percent. Most players were fibbing when they fell.

Many players claim they never dive, but chances are they have. Former England striker Michael Owen admitted that it's a bit of a gray area. "I don't think that in my career I ever actually dived," he said in an interview. "I certainly went down on occasions. Two of the biggest were against Argentina at World Cups, in 1998 and 2002. I went to the ground in situations where it would have been just about possible for me to stay on my feet."

Referees can punish dives with a yellow card. The official term for the offense is "simulation." Writer Dave Eggers said that diving is "essentially a combination of acting, lying, begging, and cheating, and these four behaviors make for an unappealing mix." At Soccer School, we don't like it either.

Target

THREE FAMOUS SOCCER FAKES

1. Roberto Rojas (Brazil vs. Chile, 1989)

The Chilean goalkeeper was banned for life after pretending that he had been injured by a firecracker that had been thrown onto the field. He dived into the smoke of the firecracker and emerged bleeding, but it turned out that he had cut himself using a razor blade in his gloves.

2. Rivaldo (Brazil vs. Turkey, 2002)

Turkish defender Hakan Ünsal kicked the ball at Rivaldo's leg, and the Brazilian midfielder fell down, clutching his face. Ünsal was sent off, but Rivaldo was later fined.

3. Arjen Robben (Netherlands vs. Mexico, 2014)

The Dutch winger apologized after trying to win a penalty by diving in the first half of a tense World Cup tie.

HOLLY WOOD

STAR STUDENT

★★★★

" Break a leg! "

STAR STUDENT **stats**

Most rolls to win a foul: 14
Different goal celebrations: 43
Bookings for playacting: 9
Most uniform changes in a game: 1
Birthplace: Broadway, Virginia
Supports: West Ham (U.K.)
Fave player: Craig Shakespeare
Trick: Inspiring team talks

DRAMA QUIZ

1. **Which of these celebrations did Stjarnan players once attempt after scoring a goal?**

   a) The Bicycle
   b) The Volcano
   c) The Cha-Cha-Cha
   d) The Moonwalk

2. **Closing your fist and keeping one thumb up is the symbol for what in most countries?**

   a) That's great.
   b) The number one
   c) Do you have any nail clippers?
   d) Look, my thumb cannot bend.

3. **What do actors traditionally say to one another before going onstage?**

   a) "Sorry for farting!"
   b) "Break a leg!"
   c) "Don't forget your lines!"
   d) "I love you, darling!"

4. **A bad actor, or one who overacts, can be called a:**

   a) Bacon
   b) Pig
   c) Ham
   d) Sausage

5. **Which masks did Gabonese forward Pierre-Emerick Aubameyang and his teammate Marco Reus wear to celebrate the striker's goal for Borussia Dortmund against rivals Schalke?**

   a) Batman and Robin
   b) Tom and Jerry
   c) Spider-Man and Superman
   d) Mickey and Minnie Mouse

Philosophers are thinkers who ask deep questions about the meaning of life. In 1637, philosopher René Descartes said, *"Cogito ergo sum,"* which is Latin for "I think, therefore I am."

Cogito ergo sum.

That's why the Soccer School motto is *"Kickito Ergo Sum,"* which is made-up Latin for "I kick, therefore I am."

Soccer School

Kickito Ergo Sum

A set of rules that guides you is called a philosophy, and you don't need to speak Latin or have been dead for centuries to have one. Ben's philosophy for life is: Be yourself; love your family; tell jokes; eat pizza; take penalties. Alex's is: Have fun; be a good friend; go cycling; do your multiplication tables; pick your nose.

Soccer players can also have philosophies for how they play. For example, a philosophy could be: Always attack; keep the ball on the ground; never dive. And coaches have sets of rules for how they approach training and tactics. In this lesson, we will tell the story of the coach Rinus Michels, whose philosophy revolutionized soccer. We'll see how the vision he had half a century ago still affects the game today.

× 6 = 24
× 6 = 30
× 6 = 36 . . .

A COACH IS BORN

Marinus "Rinus" Michels was born in Amsterdam, in the Netherlands, in 1928. He dreamed of becoming a soccer

Rinus Michels

player, and for his ninth birthday, his dad gave him his first pair of soccer cleats and the white-and-red uniform of Ajax, which at that time was a semiprofessional team.

Michels's dream came true when he was eighteen and started playing for Ajax as a center forward. In his debut game in 1946, he scored five times. He was regarded as a real team player, as he worked hard and always put his team first. Although he was thought to be a little clumsy with the ball at his feet, he always kept moving and was great at heading.

In the 269 games he played for Ajax, he scored 121 goals. He also played five games for the Netherlands before he retired with an injured back at age thirty.

With his playing career over, Michels became a gymnastics teacher at a school for deaf children. Accounts say Michels was a

NORTH SEA

TO THE U.K.

AMSTERDAM

ROTTERDAM

NETHERLANDS

GERMANY

BELGIUM

very strict teacher. During these years, he developed strategies for how to get the best out of people. Then Michels had a brainstorm: Why not combine his teaching skills and love of soccer by becoming a soccer coach? So in January 1965, when he learned that Ajax wanted a new coach, he applied for the job and got it.

When he took over as coach, Ajax was struggling in the league. But in their first game with Michels in charge, the team won 9–3. They not only avoided relegation (demotion), but also the next year went on to win the Dutch championship — and the one the year after that, and the one after that. Three in a row! In 1971, Ajax won the European Cup (the competition now called the Champions League) for the best team in Europe. No team has ever come from such a low point— either before then or since—to win this famous trophy.

THE GENERAL'S PHILOSOPHY

So how did Michels do it? He had a new approach to soccer and a new philosophy for the game. First, he was tough on his team and strict about discipline. His players nicknamed him "the General" because he set up four training sessions every day to get his team as fit as possible.

Most teams would have one or two sessions per day, not four. Michels also introduced new tactics borrowed from other countries. He made his defenders attack, as they did in Brazil, and he encouraged his players to rotate positions, as they did in Hungary. So if a midfielder moved to the wing, the winger would replace him in midfield. This versatile new way of playing became known as "total football" (using the European name for soccer). These changes had amazing results.

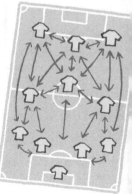

Total football

A THINKING MAN'S TROPHIES

After his success at Ajax, Michels went to coach Barcelona, in Spain, where he continued to use his innovative training methods and tactics. Under his guidance, Barcelona won the Spanish league for the first time in fourteen years.

He was then made coach of the Dutch national team. At that time, the Netherlands (often called Holland) had a mediocre team. When Michels was younger, he had played for his country, but they never won, once even losing 6–1 to Sweden. But as a coach, he turned them into one of the best teams in the world. They narrowly lost the 1974 World Cup final to West Germany. Later he led his country to the only football trophy the Netherlands has ever won: the 1988 European Championship. What an incredible achievement! In 1999, Michels was named FIFA Coach of the Century.

Michels's winning formula

Top fitness and
   discipline
         +
Attacking defenders = WINNERS
         +
Rotating positions

LASTING LEGACY

Rinus Michels is important in the history of soccer not only because he won lots of trophies but also because he left a legacy.

A legacy is something handed down through the generations, like the vase your mom is always telling you not to touch or a picture of your grandparents when they were children.

GRANDDAD → GRANDMA

It doesn't have to be an object: it can be your auntie's bad breath or, in this case, a way of doing things.

Michels's legacy is his philosophy of "total football," in which a team always has defenders who attack and players who can swap positions. Let's take a look at how the way Barcelona plays today is a consequence of Michels's work all those years ago.

HELPING FOOT

Michels had one important bit of luck when establishing his legacy. When he was coach at Ajax, his best player was the Dutch forward Johan Cruyff. It was said that Cruyff was "four-footed," because he was the first player to kick with the outside as well as the inside of his foot. Cruyff understood Michels's ideas about "total football" better than anyone. He even pointed and told his teammates where to make runs during games. Cruyff also played for Barcelona when Michels was coach there.

When Cruyff stopped playing, he also became a coach, first at Ajax and then at Barcelona, just like his former boss. At Ajax, Cruyff made sure that the team played in the Michels style. And they still do today—from the junior team right up to the senior team. At Barcelona, Cruyff did the same thing. Michels's philosophy became Cruyff's philosophy. Today the Barcelona youth academy, where Lionel Messi and many other great players were trained, still teaches its young stars to play in the way invented by Michels and continued by Cruyff. And it works.

I'M ON ALL fours!

WORLD PHILOSOPHY

In recent years, Barcelona has turned more players into coaches than any other team. Take Pep Guardiola, the Spanish midfielder, who played on the team for eleven years and went on to coach Barcelona to six trophies in a single year, 2009.

In fact, ten of Guardiola's teammates, some of whom were coached by Cruyff in 1996, became coaches at teams all over the world. Michels's original philosophy is now a global phenomenon.

Pep Guardiola was the most successful coach in Barcelona's history, winning three League titles and two Champions Leagues, as well as the Spanish Cup, the Spanish Super Cup, the UEFA Europe League Super Cup, and the Club World Cup.

 ## MICHELS'S PHILOSOPHY AROUND THE WORLD

BARCELONA 1996 PLAYER	WENT ON TO COACH . . .
Abelardo	Sporting Gijón
Guillermo Amor	Adelaide United
Sergi Barjuán	Almeria
Laurent Blanc	Bordeaux/France/PSG
Luis Enrique	Celta Vigo/Roma/Barcelona
Albert Ferrer	Real Mallorca

DUTCH DELIGHT

Another of Michels's legacies is the stunning success of Dutch soccer. The Netherlands, whose population is not even in the top ten in Europe, often does well at World Cups. Consider that England, with three times the population, did not even reach a single final in the forty-eight years after winning the World Cup in 1966. Well, the Netherlands has reached THREE finals and TWO semifinals since then.

The Netherlands also produces more successful soccer coaches than other small countries. More than fifty years after Michels first took the job as Ajax coach, his methods are still being used. That's why some people call him the inventor of modern soccer. Cruyff carried on his work, but Michels was soccer's most important philosopher.

BARCELONA 1996 PLAYER	WENT ON TO COACH . . .
Óscar García	Mac. Tel Aviv/Brighton/RB Salzburg
Pep Guardiola	Barcelona/Bayern Munich/Man. City
Julen Lopetegui	Spain Under-21s/Porto
Juan Antonio Pizzi	San Lorenzo/Valencia/Chile
Robert Prosinečki	Red Star Belgrade/Azerbaijan
Hristo Stoichkov	Bulgaria/CSKA Sofia

RIDDLE ME THIS

Johan Cruyff was also regarded as being a soccer philosopher, often because of his enigmatic or puzzling remarks. Here are five of his classic lines:

PLaying soccer is very simPLe, but pLaying simPLe soccer is the hardest.

There is onLy one baLL, so you need to have it.

If I wanted you to understand it, I would have explaine it better.

In my teams, the goaLie is the first attacker, and the striker the first defender.

Before I make a mistake, I don't make that mistake.

TULIP FEAVER

☆ STAR STUDENT

❝ Don't stand there Like a windmiLL! ❞

☆ ☆ STAR ☆ STUDENT stats

Pairs of shoes: 5
Pairs of cLogs: 15
Number of feet pLays with: 4
DaiLy intake of cheese: 1 Lb./ 5 kg
BirthpLace: Orange County, CaLifornia
SupPorts: BarceLona (Spain)
Fave pLayer: Johan Cruyff
Trick: PLays in any position

PHILOSOPHY QUIZ

1. Which philosopher came up with the line *"Cogito ergo sum"*?

a) René Descartes
b) Plato
c) Dele Alli
d) Aristotle

2. The word *philosophy* comes from two Greek words: *philo,* which means "lover of," and *sophia,* which means what?

a) Wisdom
b) Laughing
c) Girls
d) Sofas

3. Which of the following coaches has **NOT** worked as a teacher?

a) Rinus Michels
b) José Mourinho
c) Pep Guardiola
d) Louis van Gaal

4. Complete the quote by French philosopher Albert Camus: "All that I know most surely about morality and obligation, I owe to . . . "

a) Tintin
b) Goalkeepers
c) Soccer
d) Antoine Griezmann

5. Which clever man said "If you want to live a happy life, tie it to a goal, not to people or things"?

a) Albert Einstein
b) Petr Čech
c) Stephen Hawking
d) Jean-Paul Sartre

Taking photos of a soccer game is easy, right? Since all you do is point your camera at the field and press a button. Well, it's a little bit more complicated than that.

The job of a professional photographer at a match is kind of like the job of a soccer player: you need to have great technique, be fast, create chances, and have a good intuition for the game. The thrill of getting a great picture is like the thrill of scoring a great goal. In this lesson, you'll learn how to take a knockout photo. But first we need to understand just how a camera works. Smile!

LET THERE BE LIGHT

The eye is an amazing organ. When you see an object, light rays reflect off that object, pass through a **lens** at the front of your eye, and register an **image** at the back of your eye. To start with, this image is upside down. Our brains turn it the right way up—otherwise, we would get very dizzy.

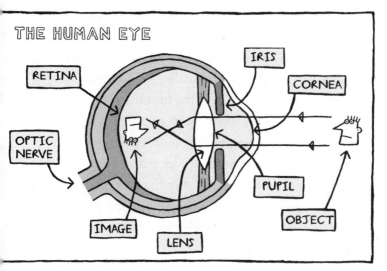

THE HUMAN EYE

RETINA — IRIS — CORNEA — OPTIC NERVE — PUPIL — IMAGE — LENS — OBJECT

A camera is a mechanical eye. The front part has a lens and the back part has a **sensor**, where the image is captured.

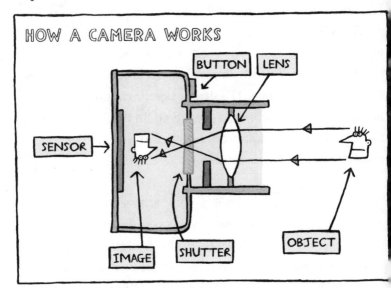

HOW A CAMERA WORKS

BUTTON LENS

SENSOR →

IMAGE SHUTTER OBJECT

The image on the back sensor is also upside down, and this time the computer in the camera turns it the right way up.

The camera also has a **shutter**, which is just in front of the back sensor. The shutter makes sure no light can get to the back. When you press the **button** on the camera, it opens the shutter for a brief moment, letting the light reach the sensor and creating the photograph.

When taking pictures of soccer players during a game, a photographer will set the shutter to open for only 1/1,600 of a second per picture. If it is open for any longer, there is a risk the players will move and the picture will be blurred.

BAG OF LENSES

Professional cameras come in two parts: the **body** (which has the sensor, the button, and the shutter) and the **lens**. This is because photographers often need to change lenses depending on what they want to shoot. Photographers at soccer games will usually have about five lenses in their bags.

A short lens is good for shooting objects that are close or to capture a big scene at a distance. A long lens is good for zooming in on objects that are far away.

SHORT
LENS

MEDIUM
LENS

LONG
LENS

The biggest lenses are just like telescopes. They are so long and heavy that photographers have to balance them on a stick to take the weight.

GAME ROUTINE

Photographers will arrive about three hours before kickoff to set up and get in position. They will be assigned a spot near the sideline, where they must stay for the length of the game.

Once the starting whistle has blown, the photographer's job is to take pictures of the *significant* moments in a game.

What are these moments? Goals, definitely; important saves; perhaps crucial fouls or tackles. These are the shots that the newspapers and websites want to have.

Like a hunter tracking an animal

through the viewfinder of a gun, most photographers will be tracking the ball through the viewfinder of their camera. Even the language of hunting and photography is similar: you *shoot* with a gun and you *shoot* with a camera.

Usually the action is where the ball is, so photographers will always be watching it. But they will also have half an eye on the rest of the field, as soccer is very fast and unpredictable.

When the ball is near the goal, the photographers will be tensing their fingers, ready to take a picture—but not just one picture. A professional sports camera has a motor attached to the button, so when you press down, it takes twelve pictures per second. *Click-click-click-click-click-click-click-click-click-click-click-click.* It's more like a machine gun than a camera.

You need to take so many photos one after another because the action is so fast, you may otherwise miss the moment when a player shoots.

If a game is exciting, photographers may take more than a thousand pictures during it, which is about a picture every five seconds. If the match is boring, they may take a hundred or so, which is about one picture a minute.

CLICK!

CLICK!

CLICK!

Once a goal has been scored, you don't need a picture of the ball in the net. All balls and all nets look the same. You want a picture of the scorer celebrating! The joyful expression on the player's face will tell the story.

CLICK!
CLICK!
CLICK!
CLICK!
CLICK!
CLICK!
CLICK!

Experienced photographers will also make sure they are aware of what is happening off the field. Sometimes the behavior of the manager on the touchline or a group of colorful fans in the stadium can make for a great photo that explains the game.

A good picture should not only capture the moment but also be in **focus** and well **framed**.

FOCUSING

When you point a camera at an object in the distance, the object will usually be blurred. The process of making the image sharp and clear is called **focusing** and involves a subtle adjustment of the lens.

Thankfully, all modern cameras have autofocus, which means that the focusing is done automatically by computer.

However, at any given time,

a camera can focus only on objects at about the same distance from it. So if there are several enthusiastic fans in the stands who are different distances away, you need to decide which one you want to have in focus. The photographer decides which part of the picture to have in focus using the viewfinder, which in Nikon cameras, for example, often looks like this.

There are 51! Count 'em!

Photographers have a choice of fifty-one parts of the image to focus on, each indicated by a little box. Using their thumb, they can move through the boxes to select the one they want.

YOU'VE BEEN FRAMED

To get a good picture, you need to be fast with your eyes, fingers, and thumbs. But it is not just about technique: a great photographer is also an artist.

If you are taking a picture of a soccer player, ideally you want them in the center of the image, or **frame**. What you don't want is the top of their head cut off, or another player in the way, or something distracting in the background.

The best photographs are like paintings. The difference is that with a painting, you can choose what you want to show. With a photograph, you can capture only what happens in front of you.

In fact, taking great soccer pictures is a real challenge. There are a lot of things to remember: getting the right lens, making sure it is in focus, framing the shot—and not missing the moment. Rob MacNeice, senior camera expert at Nikon, told us that the speed and unpredictability of the game means that Premier League soccer is one of the most difficult sports to photograph in the world.

RACE TO PUBLISH

Many cameras are now set up with wireless transmitters that send pictures as soon as they are taken to a small portable device called a dongle. From the dongle, they are transmitted via satellite to the sports desk of a newspaper or website. The picture editor will then choose the best ones to use. It can take as little as ten seconds for a picture to go from the camera to being available for everyone to see online.

PAT PARAZZI

STAR STUDENT

66 Say cheese! 99

STAR STUDENT stats

Number of lenses in bag: 6
Photo albums at home: 356
Speed of light: 671 million mph/1.1 billion kmh
Birthplace: Panorama City, California
Supports: Lens (France)
Fave player: Chris Kamara
Fave venue: Stadium of Light
Trick: Zooms around

PHOTOGRAPHY QUIZ

1. **Which of the following words also means "take a photograph"?**

a) Snap
b) Crackle
c) Pop
d) Fizz

POP!

FIZZ!

2. **How many legs does a tripod have?**

a) One
b) Two
c) Three
d) Four

3. **After Arsenal won the FA Cup in 2015, midfielder Santi Cazorla was celebrating by the goal line when he picked up a camera that had been left there by a photographer. What did he do next?**

a) He threw it into the crowd.
b) He pretended it was a ball and kicked it into the air.
c) He took a selfie of himself and his teammates.
d) He ran off with it.

4. **A paparazzo is:**

a) an Italian photographer who specializes in the Serie A soccer league.
b) a photographer who takes shots of celebrities in public places and sells them to magazines and websites.
c) an affectionate name for the oldest and most fatherly photographer at a football soccer game.
d) a photographer who takes aerial shots of soccer matches from a parachute.

5. **Digital images are made up of tiny dots called pixels. For most sports pictures in magazines, how many pixels will fit in a line 1 inch/2.5 centimeters long, like this?**

a) 50
b) 150
c) 300
d) 1000

1 in./2.5 cm

- 133 -

Male professional soccer players can be really rich. The top players at Manchester United and Real Madrid will earn more in a single week than doctors, farmers, teachers, scientists, the president, real-estate agents, gardeners, cab drivers, chefs, airline pilots, soldiers, personal trainers, dog walkers, and astronauts earn in a whole year. Why is it that being a soccer player is one of the highest-paid jobs in the world for men? In this lesson, we are going to look at how the business of soccer works and see how it has changed over the last few decades. It might be hard to imagine now, but once upon a time, soccer players earned not much at all.

BUSINESS IS A PIECE OF CAKE

Let's start by looking at why soccer players are so valuable. Over the weekend, we were at Soccer School's fall festival, and there was only one slice left at the cake stand. We both love cake and were really hungry. Let's show you what happened.

The cake went to Ben, because he could afford to pay the most. And this is just what happens in soccer. Players are like slices of cake: teams will pay as much as they have in their pockets for the slices of cake they want.

In other words, the best soccer players are amazingly well paid because their teams can afford it. If you really want something, you will pay as much as you can. So what we need to find out now is why teams have so much money

MONEY-GO-ROUND

Most businesses work on the basis that they will have money coming in (called **revenue**) and money going out (called **expenditure**).

MONEY OUT

Players' wages.

Wages of other staff, such as the coach, the chef, the person who mows the field, and the driver of the team bus.

Building the stadium and maintaining it once it is built.

MONEY IN

Tickets. Fans who want to see their team buy tickets for games, and this money goes to the team.

TV rights. Broadcasters like ESPN and Fox Sports pay money to teams for the right to show the games on their channels, because they know that fans will buy subscriptions to watch those channels or will watch in big-enough numbers to generate lots of advertising dollars.

Sponsorship. Companies pay money to teams to put their brand names on the teams' shirts or on the stadium, in order to get the brands seen by as many people as possible.

Merchandising. Fans buy official replica shirts, key rings, mugs, calendars, and other licensed products, and some of this money goes back to the team.

Winning competitions. Teams that win the Premier League or the CONCACAF Champions League get cash as well as a trophy.

Gifts. Some teams have rich owners who will often dip into their own pockets to help out their team.

If you exclude gifts from owners and cash from trophies, all revenue ultimately comes from fans.

Ka-ching!
Ka-ching!
Ka-ching!

When we go to a game, we hand over money.

When we buy pajamas with our team's logo, we hand over money.

When we subscribe to a cable sports channel, we hand over money.

Soccer fans might not be rich, but there are millions of us. If we all pay small amounts through tickets, cable subscriptions, and team shirts, then it soon adds up. Teams have lots of money because of you and me. The money leaves our pockets and eventually arrives in players' pockets.

THE RICH GET RICHER

In business, if you have money already, it is usually easier to make more money.

The richest teams have the most money, so they can build the biggest stadiums. If they have the biggest stadiums, they can sell the most tickets. If they sell the most tickets, they make the most money. So they get even richer.

SUCCESS BREEDS SUCCESS

In soccer, if you have the best players already, it is usually easier to continue to buy the best players.

The richest teams can afford the best players, so they have the best chance of winning trophies. The more trophies a team wins, the more prize money they get and the more TV money they get (because they will be shown on TV more often). So they will remain one of the richest teams and will continue to be able to buy the best players.

MODERN MILLIONAIRES

You might assume that top soccer players have always lived in mansions, driven expensive cars, and worn snazzy clothes. But it's not true. The millionaire player is a recent phenomenon. Until 1961, English players were allowed to earn only up to £20 a week, or about $600 a week in today's dollars, less than what an elementary-school teacher earns.

The players were so angry about being paid so little that they threatened to stop playing unless they were

allowed more money. The League caved in to the players'
demands, and as soon as the £20-a-week limit was lifted,
Johnny Haynes of Fulham became the best-paid player in
the country, earning £100 a week (about $3,000 today). In the
United States, men's soccer players' salaries have skyrocketed
in the last decade. The average annual salary for a Major

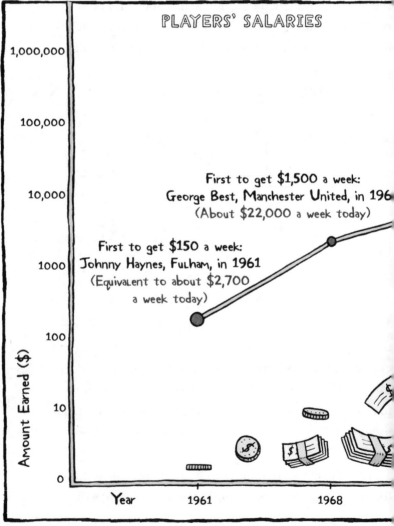

PLAYERS' SALARIES

First to get $1,500 a week:
George Best, Manchester United, in 196
(About $22,000 a week today)

First to get $150 a week:
Johnny Haynes, Fulham, in 1961
(Equivalent to about $2,700
a week today)

Amount Earned ($)

Year   1961   1968

League Soccer player has gone from about $100,000 in 2007 to an average of more than $300,000 now. More than twenty MLS players take home more than $1 million a year.

Here is a graph that shows the highest-earning players of their day. The growth has been incredible: Ronaldo earns about five hundred times what Haynes did in 1961.

First to get over $1,000,000 a week (including sponsorship deals): Cristiano Ronaldo, Real Madrid, in 2016

First to get 5,000 a week: , Roma, in 1980 out $65,000 week today)

First to get $150,000 a week: Sol Campbell, Arsenal, in 2001 (About $225,000 a week today)

1980   2001   Today

Wages have risen so fast because there is now much more money in soccer. There are a few reasons for this:

1. Ticket prices have gone up and stadiums are bigger, so teams make more money on game days.

2. The money paid to teams for TV rights has increased massively. TV companies can afford to pay teams more, using the income from fans' subscriptions and charging top dollar for ad time.

3. More soccer is shown on TV, with audiences watching all around the world. This has raised the profile of the game, and teams can now earn more money for sponsorship and merchandising deals.

RICH LISZT

STAR STUDENT

"Ka-ching!"

STAR STUDENT stats

Cars in garage: 12
Toy cars in playroom: 400
Number of staff: 20
Annual yield: 32 percent
Birthplace: Tenerife, Spain
Supports: Fortuna Sittard (Netherlands)
Fave player: Raheem Sterling
Trick: Always has a coin in his pocket, even if the referee
☆ doesn't

BUSINESS STUDIES QUIZ

1. What is the currency in Spain?

a) The tortilla
b) The Spanish dollar
c) The peseta
d) The euro

2. If a soccer player earns $1,000,000 in a week, how much does he earn per second?

a) 0.16 cents
b) 1.6 cents
c) 16 cents
d) $1.65

3. List the following from richest to poorest:

a) World's richest soccer player
b) World's richest boxer
c) World's richest movie star
d) World's richest banker

4. Manchester City is owned by Sheikh Mansour, one of the richest men in the world. Where is he from?

a) United Arab Emirates
b) Hong Kong
c) Egypt
d) Saudi Arabia

5. What did Cristiano Ronaldo, the highest-earning athlete in the world, buy for his agent, Jorge Mendes, as a wedding present?

a) A copy of Soccer School
b) A pair of Mr. and Mrs. pillowcases
c) A Real Madrid season ticket
d) A Greek island

The Blues! The Reds! The Whites! The Yellows!

No, we're not talking about Ben's collection of felt-tip pens, but about soccer teams and their shirts. Shirt color is such an important part of a team's identity that fans often use it as a nickname for the team. In this lesson, we will learn how some famous teams gained their distinctive colors.

And we'll look at national uniforms too. Why is it that some countries play in the colors of their national flag but others don't? Behind every shirt, there is a colorful story. But first we need to go back in time to the game's early days.

SOCCER CAPS

In the middle of the nineteenth century, when modern soccer came into being in England, teams didn't wear a standard uniform, or "kit," as it is called there. Instead, players wore whatever they had. In order to tell the teams apart, the players wore different-colored caps on their heads or sashes over their shirts.

But this could get confusing—imagine what would happen if everyone's cap fell off!

Excuse me, sir, are you on my team?

In the 1860s, the first English soccer teams were founded. Over the next ten years, they decided that their players would wear colored shirts. Many took their team colors from schools—either schools the founders had attended or those with teams they admired.

Blackburn Rovers, for example, based the half-and-half style of their uniform on that of Malvern College, a school in Worcestershire.

COPY-KITS

Most early uniforms were colors such as white, black, blue, or red because they were cheaper to buy. Teams that were founded later on often based their uniforms on those of other, more established teams.

TEAM	COLORS	INSPIRED BY
Arsenal	red shirts	Nottingham Forest
Athletic Bilbao	red/white stripes	Southampton
Juventus	black/white stripes	Notts County
Leeds	white	Real Madrid

CROSBY TO CATALONIA

There's a story behind the color of every team's uniform. Look at the history of Barcelona's blue-and-red shirts. It's actually two stories, since no one knows which is correct.

Our first story begins in Crosby, a town in England, at the end of the nineteenth century. It's home to a famous school called Merchant Taylors'. The school's coat of arms has a lion on a blue background surrounded by red ornamental features. Note the colors: blue and red.

Sports-mad brothers Arthur and Ernest Witty went to school at Merchant Taylors'. After they left school, they moved to Barcelona, Spain, where their dad ran a shipping company. Soon after October 1899, they became involved with a new soccer team called Barcelona. Their dad's company imported leather balls, nets, and referees' whistles from England for the team to use.

Both Arthur and Ernest played for Barcelona, and Arthur became the team president. And when the team had to decide on the color of their uniform, they picked . . . blue and red! It seems the Witty brothers chose their old school colors for Barcelona.

The team was not well known at the time, but it later became one of the most successful teams in the world, winning La Liga, the top Spanish league, and the Champions League, the European championship, many times. Barcelona's red-and-blue shirts are one of the most recognizable uniforms in sports, and they might have come from the colors of a school in the north of England.

But now for our second story. The other explanation for Barcelona's uniform is that the Swiss founder of the team, who grew up in Basel, Switzerland, based it on Basel's colors—which are also blue and red.

Historians will debate the origins of this iconic uniform until the end of time. But here at Soccer School, we like to think that the real inspiration was Merchant Taylors'. We schools have got to stick together!

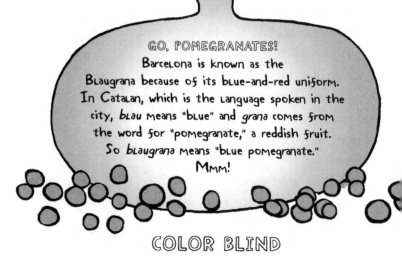

GO, POMEGRANATES!
Barcelona is known as the Blaugrana because of its blue-and-red uniform. In Catalan, which is the language spoken in the city, *blau* means "blue" and *grana* comes from the word for "pomegranate," a reddish fruit. So *blaugrana* means "blue pomegranate." Mmm!

COLOR BLIND

As we've just seen, uniforms are an important part of a team's identity. Fans can feel very protective of their team's colors. Just look at what happened to Cardiff City a few years ago.

In May 2010, Vincent Tan, a wealthy businessman from Malaysia, bought Cardiff City. Fans were very excited because he promised to spend lots of money to help the team get promoted to the Premier League.

But he had a condition: he wanted to change Cardiff's uniform from blue to red. Now, Cardiff City had worn blue since they first took that name in 1908. Not only that,

but they had a bluebird on their team logo, and their nickname was the Bluebirds.

Tan had a proposal about that too. He wanted to change the bluebird to a dragon. And his reason for all of this? Tan said his lucky color was red, which is associated with success in Asia.

Most fans protested, but Tan got his way. He spent about £70 million on the team, and Cardiff City started playing in red. Some supporters were so angry that they stopped going to games. But Tan's plan worked, and Cardiff was promoted to the Premier League.

Then their fortunes changed again. They won only seven matches in the Premier League and finished at the bottom of the standings. Six months after relegation, or demotion to a lower league, Tan switched the uniform back to blue and reinstated the bluebird on the team logo. He claimed his mother had reminded him of the importance of "togetherness, unity, and happiness." The team might not have been winning as much, but at least the fans were happy again.

VISIONS OF BLUE

Cardiff City is known as the Bluebirds. Many other teams are simply nicknamed the Blues:

And some national teams too:

France
(Les Bleus)
Italy
(Azzurri)

Birmingham City
Chelsea
Everton
Ipswich Town
Shrewsbury Town
Southend United
Wycombe Wanderers

Come on, you Blues!

WE'RE FLAGGING

But how do national teams decide what colors to wear? Most of them wear the colors of their country's flag.

This trend started with the first-ever international game, between England and Scotland in 1872. England wore white shirts to match the background color of their flag, which is called the Saint George's Cross. Scotland wore blue shirts to match the background color of their flag, which is called the Saint Andrew's Cross.

England and Scotland still wear these colors. England also usually wears blue shorts, because according to English Football Association historian David Barber, blue was the FA's official color. The three lions on England's logo are blue for the same reason. But who has ever seen a blue lion before?

OFF-COLOR COUNTRIES

Some national uniforms don't reflect the colors of their flag at all, which can be confusing.

The Netherlands' flag is red, white, and blue, but they wear orange. Italy's flag is red, white, and green, but they wear blue. Were their uniform designers color-blind? Not quite . . .

Both uniforms make reference to old rulers. For the Netherlands, it is William of Orange, who led a Dutch revolt against Spanish rule in 1568 that resulted in the Netherlands' independence in 1648. Funnily enough, even though William of Orange is a national hero, the town of Orange that his name refers to is hundreds of miles from the Netherlands, in France. Even funnier, this Orange has nothing to do with the color orange. It was originally named Arausio by the ancient Romans, after an ancient water god, and over time became the word *orange*. Those Dutch used a bit of artistic license!

For Italy, their blue uniform comes from one of the oldest royal families in the world, the Casa Savoia, who ruled from 1861 until 1946. Blue was their official color, while their coat of arms, a white cross on a red background, was the logo on Italy's uniform at the 1934 World Cup. Here are some other countries whose uniforms don't match their flags:

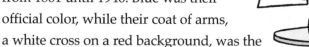

TEAM	UNIFORM	FLAG
Australia	green/gold	blue/white/red
Germany	white	black/red/yellow
India	blue	orange/white/green
Japan	blue	white/red
Slovenia	green/white	red/white/blue

ROY G. BIV

☆ STAR STUDENT

"Lighten up, man!"

☆☆ STAR STUDENT stats

Primary colors: 3
Main colors in rainbow: 7
Shirts in collection: 342
Crayons in desk: 25
Birthplace: Yellowstone National Park
Supports: Suwon Samsung Bluewings (South Korea)
Fave player: Jamie Redknapp
Trick: Dazzling ball skills

FASHION QUIZ

1. What fruit is associated with the uniform color of Barcelona?

a) Pineapple
b) Pomegranate
c) Raspberry
d) Clementine

2. Who lives in the White House?

a The queen of England
b) The president of the United States
c) England's soccer-team manager
d) Cristiano Ronaldo

3. What two colors do poetry experts say have no words to rhyme with them?

a) Turquoise and blue
b) Copper and sienna
c) Fuchsia and yellow
d) Orange and purple

4. Which Italian team produced a green-and-gray-camouflage away uniform in 2013?

a) Bologna
b) Perugia
c) Napoli
d) Torino

5. Which goalkeeper designed his own fluorescent uniform to wear at the 1994 World Cup?

a) Jorge Campos (Mexico)
b) Claudio Taffarel (Brazil)
c) Bogdan Stelea (Romania)
d) Joseph-Antoine Bell (Cameroon)

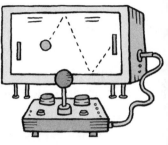

Being a top soccer player is often really boring. You have lots of time with nothing to do. You spend hours on buses and planes to and from games and hours in hotel rooms for away games or international tournaments. So it's not surprising that players like playing video games. Whenever we speak to players, they always tell us that it's their favorite way to relax and unwind. And even though they play real soccer almost every day, professional players also love to play soccer-based video games.

In this lesson, we're going to learn about computers and how you can turn soccer players, with all their individual skills, into video game characters.

We will also find out if playing video games can make you a better player. But you need to be careful—sometimes it can have a negative effect on your game. At Inter Milan, Swedish striker Zlatan Ibrahimović used to play video games for ten hours at a stretch. We suspect that it caused a drop in his performances. And when former England keeper David James let in three goals in one match, he blamed it on too much PlayStation. "I was getting carried away playing [it] for hours on end," he said.

NUMBERS GAME

A computer is an electronic machine that carries out tasks when you give it a **program**, or set of instructions. Computers store information using only the digits 0 and 1, which are called binary digits, or **bits**. A group of eight bits is called a **byte**.

Video games are a type of program, which means they are made up of bytes. The information contained in the game *Worldwide Soccer Manager* amounts to well over a **gigabyte**, which is a billion bytes. That's a lot of 0s and 1s.

In *Worldwide Soccer Manager*, you are the coach of a team and you pick computer versions of real players for your team, which then plays against other teams. You decide which players to pick based on their individual strengths and characteristics.

What's exciting is that *Worldwide Soccer Manager* is very realistic. Players perform just like they do in real life. To do this, the game stores lots of information about each player as a set of numbers, which are then translated into bytes.

The numbers that define each player's characteristics are scores out of 20. Players are scored on more than 250 qualities, such as:

- *ability*
- *acceleration*
- *adaptability*
- *ambition*
- *anticipation*
- *concentration*
- *corners*

- *crossing*
- *decisions*
- *dirtiness*
- *dribbling*
- *first touch*
- *flair*
- *free kicks*

- *heading*
- *injury*
- *jumping ability*
- *leadership*
- *loyalty*
- *marking*
- *natural fitness*

- *passing*
- *potential ability*
- *pressure*
- *professionalism*
- *proneness*
- *stamina*
- *strength*
- *tackling*
- *teamwork*
- *technique*
- *versatility*
- *vision*
- *work rate*

Once you start thinking about it, you see that the list of qualities that make a good soccer player is a very long one.

When your player faces an opponent during a game, the game program uses an **algorithm**—a step-by-step process—that decides what will happen next by comparing each player's numbers.

Worldwide Soccer Manager does this in more than 250 categories, almost instantaneously, during every moment of the game. That's what makes it feel so realistic.

Alex	QUALITIES	Ben
10	Dress sense	15
20	Hairiness	7
6	Eating speed	19
12	Dance technique	12
19	Sense of humor	18
17	Fart power	4
1	Skill at spreading jam	20
5	Competence at walking dogs	20

QUALITY CONTROL

For *Worldwide Soccer Manager* to be true to life, it needs to have the best data possible. The game has a network of 1,300 scouts, all around the world, who watch the real-life players closely so they can be as accurate as possible when they score them out of 20 for the game.

If a player always wears the captain's armband and their teammates look up to them, they might score 20 on leadership. If they can barely lift off the ground when they jump, they might score a 1 on jumping ability.

But some qualities are more difficult to judge. How do you measure skill, ambition, heart, or versatility? Or how much of an oddball a player is?

BEST

LEAP

FOR

HEADERS

MOST APPEARANCES AS A SUB

LEA DER

12

Worldwide Soccer Manager gives goalkeepers a rating for eccentricity. It's a soccer cliché that goalkeepers are off their rockers. Many great keepers have been notable characters, such as the Colombian René Higuita, who invented the scorpion kick, and the Liverpool hero Bruce Grobbelaar, who wobbled his legs to distract opponents during the 1984 European Cup final penalty shoot-out. Here are five cuckoo keepers.

NAME	COUNTRY	WACKINESS
Fabien Barthez	France	Teammates would kiss his bald head before France games at the 1998 World Cup.
José Luis Chilavert	Paraguay	Scored free kicks and penalties when not defending his goal.
Hugo Gatti	Argentina	Would pat strikers on the head after catching crosses.
René Higuita	Colombia	Invented the scorpion kick, a clearance with the heels after a somersault.
Jens Lehmann	Germany	Once appeared to pee behind the goal and borrowed a fan's glasses.

CUCKOO-EST KEEPER

WORST CORNER TAKER

FAMOUS FANS

When professional soccer players play soccer video games, they are in the weird position of being able to pick computer versions of themselves for their teams.

French midfielder Paul Pogba was playing for Juventus when he appointed himself as manager of Chelsea on *Worldwide Soccer Manager*. One signing he made was a French midfielder named . . . Paul Pogba. Was this an indication he wanted to move to Chelsea in real life? Pogba's *Worldwide Soccer Manager* team was made public when the French Football Federation released footage of Pogba playing the game on its YouTube channel. It was actually a bit embarrassing for Pogba, because he'd dropped Chelsea's captain at the time, English defender John Terry, and picked only three of his Juventus teammates to play alongside him at Chelsea. Awkward!

Norwegian striker Ole Gunnar Solskjær, who once scored in the Champions League final for Manchester United, always wanted to become a coach. In preparation, he played *Worldwide Soccer Manager*, which he said taught him a lot about young players and management. When he finally did become a coach at Molde, his hometown club in Norway, he won the league in his first season.

TRAIN THE BRAIN

Video games are fun—but can they make you a better soccer player?

The training staff at Manchester United thought so. They asked their players to play a game called *NeuroTracker*, where eight balls bounce around a screen. The aim is to follow four of the balls without getting distracted by the others. At the beginning of the session, the players are told which four balls to follow, and at the end, they are asked to point them out again. They get top scores if they get all four correct.

This game sounds pretty boring—there are no racing cars or battles or monsters—but it is believed to improve concentration, focus, and spatial awareness and sharpen reactions, all qualities that are required to be a good player.

Scientists are divided about whether "brain-training" video games like this one really can make you a better player. These games may well improve reaction times and motor skills—and will, of course, make you better at following four balls around a screen—but whether this is useful when playing in front of ninety thousand fans at Wembley Stadium, no one yet knows. Even if Manchester United was hoping so!

RATINGS RELEGATION

An English Premier League player once complained to the makers of a soccer video game because he felt his ratings in the game were unfairly low. He said that locker-room morale was affected by it. But the video-game company held firm and did not change his ratings. It was the right decision: the team finished bottom of the league and was relegated.

Attributes	Rating
Tackling	2
Shooting	8
Teamwork	5
Moaning	98
Complaining	100

JOY STICK

☆ STAR STUDENT

"Let's reboot!"

☆☆☆ STAR STUDENT stats

Facebook friends: 121,395
Memory: 1 trillion gigabytes
Voltage: 24V
Hours playing Minecraft every day: 3 1/2
Birthplace: Silicon Valley, California
Supports: Metalist Kharkiv (Ukraine)
Fave player: Mix Diskerud
☆ Trick: Can freeze her position

COMPUTER SCIENCE QUIZ

1. What is a megabyte?

a) A cool byte

b) A triple-decker sandwich

c) Something a shark does

d) A million bytes

2. Which of the following attributes is useful for a soccer player?

a) Sense of smell

b) Musical taste

c) Loyalty

d) Likes animals

3. Which player spent three hours in the afternoon playing a soccer computer game before scoring in the World Cup final that night?

a) Ronaldo (Brazil, 2002)

b) Andrea Pirlo (Italy, 2006)

c) Andrés Iniesta (Spain, 2010)

d) Mario Götze (Germany, 2014)

4. Which team does the man who created the *Worldwide Soccer Manager* game support?

a) Watford

b) Arsenal

c) Chelsea

d) West Ham

5. What was unique about the video game *FIFA 16*?

a) You could change the hairstyles of players.

b) Players got injured during goal celebrations.

c) One of the available tactical systems used ten forwards.

d) It featured women's teams for the first time.

Soccer has an amazing capacity to bring people together.

Like when you make friends kicking a ball around in the park. Like when you meet someone who supports the same team as you and become friends for life. Like when the country goes soccer-crazy during the World Cup.

But soccer can also push people apart.

In this lesson, we will see how the game can bring countries together and also create tensions between them. Because when two countries face each other, the match can be about more than just eleven players versus eleven players. It is about the collective hopes and fears of each nation.

Matters concerning how countries are run and how they get along with one another are what we call politics. Soccer can impact politics—sometimes for the good and sometimes for the bad.

CHRISTMAS TRUCE

The First World War lasted from 1914 to 1918 and involved some of the most powerful countries in the world at the time, with many others also joining in. Germany was on one side and the United Kingdom, France, and Russia were on the other.

The main battlefield in Europe consisted of two lines of ditches, known as **trenches**, which ran alongside each other for hundreds of miles. British and French Allied soldiers lived in the trenches on one side, and German soldiers lived in the trenches on the other side. Between the two lines was an area called **no-man's-land**, which was covered in barbed wire and was sometimes only a few dozen yards wide. Soldiers who stepped onto no man's land would be immediately shot at by the enemy.

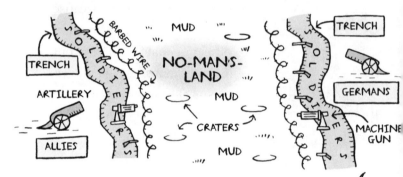

Life in the trenches was miserable and dangerous. They were dirty, cold, and infested by rat, and the soldiers were constantly shaken by the thunder of guns and bombs. In December 1914, the German High Command sent Christmas trees to their trenches to cheer the soldiers up. A short distance away in the British trenches, the soldiers

were also missing home and their families. When the Germans sang the Christmas carol "Silent Night" ("Stille Nacht" in German), British soldiers heard them, applauded, and asked for more.

On Christmas Day 1914, an incredible thing happened. In some of the trenches, British and German soldiers put down their weapons and walked into no-man's-land. But they didn't attack each other. Instead, they shook hands, exchanged gifts, and

decided to play soccer together. The games were chaotic. The soldiers' boots were heavy, the leather ball soon got soggy, and goalposts were caps or helmets. Even more confusingly, some of the games along the trenches were one-hundred-a-side.

After the Christmas period, the soldiers returned to their trenches and the war continued as before. By the end of the war, the total number of soldiers who died was about eleven million. The Christmas Truce of 1914 represented a moment of togetherness during one of the darkest times in European history. When they played each other at soccer, the British and the Germans were not enemies but friends.

SYMBOL OF PEACE

Something similar happened between the United States and Iran during the 1998 World Cup, in France. The governments of the two countries used to be on good terms, but in 1979 the Iranian leader was overthrown and a new government took control. This Iranian leadership did not like the United States, and the two nations entered a period of hostility and distrust. When they were both drawn in the same group at the World Cup, FIFA was worried that bad feelings and threats would overshadow the game.

Thankfully the game passed peacefully. The Iranian team gave each American player a bouquet of white roses, a symbol of peace in Iran, before kickoff. Iran won the game 2–1, but the impact went beyond the result. "We did more in ninety minutes than the politicians did in twenty years," said U.S. defender Jeff Agoos.

Things went so well, in fact, that the two countries played a friendly game against each other eighteen months later in California. "[That] was far more significant because . . . it needed the cooperation of both sides," said Mehrdad Masoudi, who worked with the Iran team at the World Cup fixture. "But it could only have happened if the match at France '98 was a success."

FIGHTING TALK

Here at Soccer School, we don't like war. It is a nasty activity that pits people against one another with horrific and tragic consequences.

Even so, have you noticed that the words and phrases we use to talk about soccer are very similar to those we use to describe a war? Commentators, coaches, and players talk so much about enemies, plans of attack, and glory that they sound like army generals:

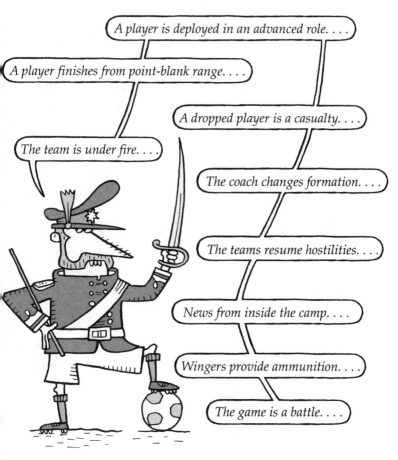

A player is deployed in an advanced role. . . .

A player finishes from point-blank range. . . .

A dropped player is a casualty. . . .

The team is under fire. . . .

The coach changes formation. . . .

The teams resume hostilities. . . .

News from inside the camp. . . .

Wingers provide ammunition. . . .

The game is a battle. . . .

SPORTING REGALIA

Another parallel between soccer and war is that both soccer players and soldiers wear special clothes to do their jobs. Soccer players and soldiers both wear uniforms, and for much the same reasons, too:

ARMY UNIFORM	SOCCER UNIFORM	PURPOSE
Chevrons on arm	Armband	To denote authority
Armor	Shin pads	For protection
Medals	Star for World Cup victory	To represent past honors
Insignia	Logo	To denote team/regiment

And there are other similarities between the world of a soldier and that of a soccer player:

SOLDIER	SOCCER PLAYER	PURPOSE
Rosettes/scarves	Rosettes/scarves	To show allegiance
Flag	Fan banner	To show allegiance
General in control room	Coach in dugout	To give orders
Marching tune	Fans' chant	To improve morale
Animal on a standard	Three Lions	A mascot to defend

In international soccer, the link between soccer and war is even more apparent. National teams stir up strong feelings and can rekindle historical resentments toward other countries. In one famous case, three World Cup qualifying games served as a tipping point for a short but deadly war.

THE SOCCER WAR

In 1969, Honduras and El Salvador faced each other in qualifiers for the 1970 World Cup. The countries are neighbors in Central America and were already bickering like brothers and sisters about all sorts of

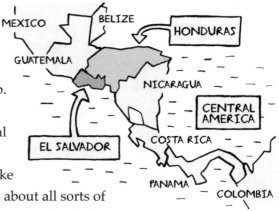

issues. The three games made relations worse.

The first game was in Honduras. Newspapers reported that in order to stop the El Salvador team from getting a good night's sleep, Honduran fans deliberately made lots of noise outside the team's hotel. After Honduras won 1–0, fans fought one another in the stadium.

The atmosphere was even more tense for the return game in El Salvador. The Salvadorans smashed the windows of the hotel where the Honduras team was staying and threw rotten eggs and dead rats through them. Fans had burned the Honduras flag, so when their national anthem was played, a dirty dishcloth was run up the stadium flagpole instead. During the match, the field was lined with soldiers holding guns. El Salvador won the game 3–0, causing riots of jubilation in the streets.

With one win each, there was to be a decider. Because of the escalating violence between the supporters of both teams, it was decided that the game would be played in another country—Mexico. The game was hard-fought, and El Salvador scored in extra time to win 3–2.

Less than three weeks later, the countries were at war. Salvadoran planes bombed Honduras, and the Salvadoran army invaded. The war lasted four days (or one hundred hours) and cost the lives of about three thousand people, mostly civilians.

Even though the roots of the conflict were to do with things like jobs and migration and trade, the decision to go to war was a result of the fervent **patriotism** (love for your country) stoked up by the World Cup qualifiers. For that reason, the episode is now known as the Soccer War.

El Salvador didn't win a game, or score a goal, at the 197 World Cup.

BATTLE FOR PEACE

But soccer can help bring about peace, too. It's the job of politicians to run countries—bu sometimes they need a little bit of help.

In Ivory Coast, the striker Didier Drogb played an important role in ending a war between rival faction in his country. Drogba is Ivory Coast's most

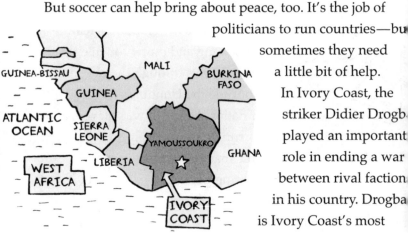

famous player. He was African Footballer of the Year twice and scored 104 goals for Chelsea.

In 2002, a **civil war** started in Ivory Coast. A civil war means that people in the same country are fighting one another, and in Ivory Coast hundreds, if not thousands, had died. But also, in 2005, the country qualified to play in the World Cup for the first time.

Ivory Coast's final qualifying match for the 2006 World Cup saw them win against Sudan. As soon as the end-of-game whistle blew, the players, who were all from different parts of Ivory Coast, celebrated with one another, hugging and dancing.

In the locker room afterward, Drogba gave a live TV interview. "Men and women of Ivory Coast, from the north, south, center, and west," he said, "we proved today that all Ivorians can coexist and play together with a shared aim, to qualify for the World Cup. We promised you that the celebration would unite the people."

The players all went down on their knees. Drogba, from the south, was embraced by his teammate Kolo Touré, from the north. *"Pardonnez!"* Drogba said. It means "Forgive!" in French. *"Pardonnez! Pardonnez!* Please lay down your weapons. Hold elections. All will be better."

His words helped bring the whole country together and made the warring factions listen to each other. It was reported that Drogba then spent months behind the scenes persuading the two sides to talk.

"Drogba [was] involved in lots of quiet, but successful, soccer diplomacy," said a report about soccer's role in bringing peace to Africa. "He personally intervened to convince [the opposing sides] to agree [to a peace treaty]."

Drogba said later, "I have won many trophies in my time, but nothing will ever top helping win the battle for peace in my country."

POLLY TICKS

STAR STUDENT

"Let's vote on it!"

STAR STUDENT stats

Flags in collection: 136
Votes: 12 million
Length of term: 4 years
Birthplace: Westminster, England
Supports: New England Revolution (United States)
Fave player: Whoever is captain
Trick: Negotiating with the referee

POLITICAL SCIENCE QUIZ

1. On what special day in 1914 did German and British soldiers lay down weapons and play soccer with each other?

a) New Year's Day
b) Easter Sunday
c) Christmas Day
d) Alex's birthday

2. What military command do coaches often shout at strikers?

a) "Stand at attention!"
b) "Take cover!"
c) "Shoot!"
d) "Form a phalanx!"

3. In which country did the boss of the biggest soccer team become president?

a) Argentina
b) Germany
c) Russia
d) The United States

4. Which team does England's Prince William, who is president of the English Football Association, support?

a) Aston Villa
b) Crystal Palace
c) Queens Park Rangers
d) Newcastle United

5. Argentinian forward Diego Maradona claimed his goal against England in the 1986 World Cup was "divine revenge" for the Falklands War. But what did "God" use to score?

a) The Head of God
b) The Foot of God
c) The Hand of God
d) The Backheel of God

Friday
Periods 3rd + 4th

MUSIC

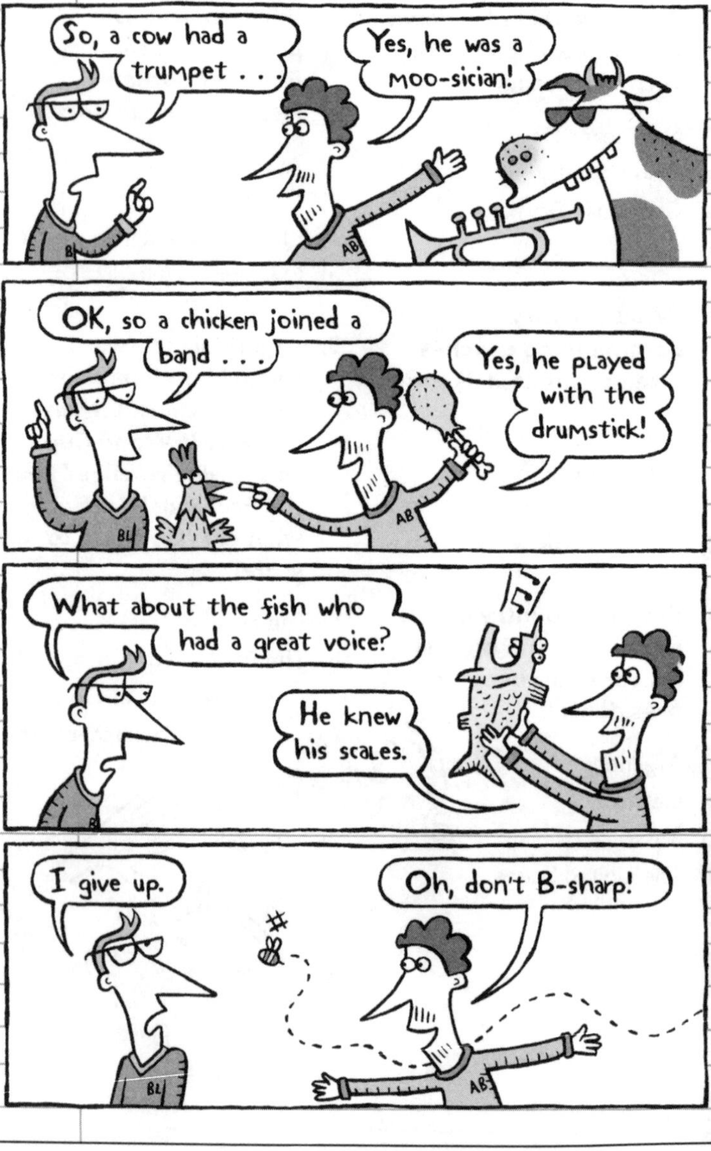

'Ere we go, 'ere we go, 'ere we gooooo!

Doesn't a sing-a-long make the world seem like a better place? It certainly makes soccer more fun to watch.

Soccer songs—or chants—are as old as the game itself. Singing brings the fans and the team together. Fans feel part of something bigger than themselves, and the team feels the support. Coaches sometimes say that the loud singing of fans plays a part in a victory. After all, players are just like everyone else and respond better to cheers than boos. Imagine if *you* were playing soccer and someone booed every time you touched the ball. It would be hard to concentrate.

In this lesson, we will find out where soccer chants come from and why we sing them. We'll see how in some ways they are similar to ancient Greek poetry—although luckily we don't have to sing them in Greek.

We will also look at national anthems, which are sung before every international match played between two different countries. National anthems often reflect the personality of a whole country, and fans love to sing them as loudly as possible. Sometimes the players join in, and sometimes they don't. At Soccer School, we want everyone to sing along, whatever the tune—this lesson is going to be a noisy one!

FAN FOLK

Thousands of soccer songs have been written over the years, and singing at games has become the norm. But there is no committee that meets during a game and decides what songs will be sung. There is no elected songwriter who writes or sings the funniest tunes of the day. Instead, anyone who has a song they want to sing simply stands up and sings it. If other people like it, they join in.

Some people see these songs as a form of **folk music**. Folk music usually has no known composer and is passed from person to person by listening and repeating. This method of sharing was how some of the world's first poems came to be heard. The *Iliad* and the *Odyssey*, which are believed to have been composed by the ancient Greek poet Homer, date back nearly three thousand years. These epic poems weren't originally written down but were passed from person to person by word of mouth, much like some of the most memorable soccer songs.

STAND UP . . . IF YOU LOVE HOMER . .

STEADY ON

The oldest soccer song that can still be heard in the stands today was written in the 1890s for a local factory team on England's east coast. It became the official song of nearby Norwich City when the team was founded, in 1902. Today, more than a century later, Norwich fans still sing it before every game.

On the Ball, City
Kick it off,
Throw it in,
Have a little scrimmage,
Keep it low,
A splendid rush,
Bravo, win or die;
On the ball, City,
Never mind the danger,
Steady on,
Now's your chance,
Hurrah! We've scored a goal.
City, City, City.

Rousing stuff or what?

The word *scrimmage* means "struggle." It is used in different sports, most famously in rugby, where it gave us the word *scrum*. It can also mean "a practice match."

WHAT A TUNE

Soccer brings people together. If you are singing the same song as thousands of other fans, you feel close to them, even if you don't know them. Celebrating your support for a team, even if they are losing, can be a joyful experience. The tunes of the songs are often well-known melodies or borrowed from recent pop songs.

CHANT ORIGINS

Chant: *"Stand up if you hate [opposition team]!"*
Sung by: Almost every European team about their rivals
Original song: "Go West" by the Village People (1979)
Meaning: The original song is understood as a gay anthem celebrating San Francisco as a place of freedom. It became more popular in 1993, when the English group the Pet Shop Boys released their version.

Chant: *"One [name of player], there's only one [name of player]. . . ."*
Sung by: Almost every team about their star player
Original song: "Guantanamera" by Joseíto Fernández (1920s)
Meaning: This Cuban song was written about a man who fell in love with a woman from Guantánamo after she made him a steak sandwich. The Sandpipers, an American band, reworked it in 1966, and it became an international hit.

Chant: *"You'll never walk alone . . . ."*
Sung by: Liverpool, Celtic, Club Brugge, Tokyo, Borussia Dortmund
Original song: "You'll Never Walk Alone" by Rodgers and Hammerstein (1945)
Meaning: The song first appeared in the musical *Carousel.* It was sung to a woman after her husband killed himself by falling on his knife while trying to escape capture after a robbery. Liverpool-based band Gerry and the Pacemakers covered it in 1963, and it became an anthem for Liverpool and many other teams.

Soccer songs can also be funny. Fans of Spanish side Cádiz always sing, "Referee, you're gorgeous!" just to be different from all those who usually complain about referees. Humor is a big

Jimmy is great at conducting the midfield.

part of soccer chants, and often the most popular songs are the funniest ones.

The Soccer School team needs a song. If you have any ideas, let us know!

NATIONAL ANTHEMS

At international games, teams sing their country's **national anthem**, a piece of music recognized by the people and the government as the official song of the country.

The tune of the U.S. anthem, "The Star-Spangled Banner," came from a song first heard in 1773 at the Anacreontic Society, an English men's social club named after Anacreon, a Greek poet who wrote about love and wine. The song, "To Anacreon in Heaven," was famously difficult to sing; one solo singer would try to hit all the high notes before everyone else in the club would join in for the chorus. The song soon became popular outside of the society, with dozens of different words written for the tune. The words to "The Star-Spangled Banner" were from an 1814 poem called "Defence of Fort M'Henry." It was confirmed as the national anthem by President Herbert Hoover in 1931.

Most national anthems became official only in the 1920s. They tend to fall into five types:

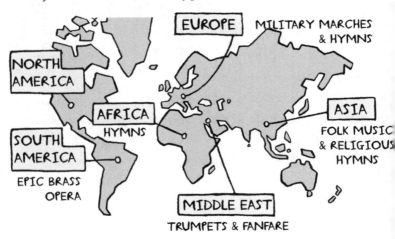

The anthems in North America combine each of these types. Most fans love to sing the national anthem before an international match, but not all players do. Sometimes they stay silent, preferring to save their energy and focus on the game. Some have no option: Spain's national anthem has no words. The anthems of Uruguay and Argentina have long musical sections before the words begin, but because FIFA allows only ninety seconds for each anthem, the players often sing the words to the wrong tune.

Players have been criticized for not singing their national anthem. Some people think it means that they don't care about their country. Germany's team at the 2010 World Cup came under fire for not singing their national anthem, and the England coach at the time, Roy Hodgson, told his players they had to join in with "God Save the Queen" before matches at the 2014 World Cup. Singing didn't help England then: they may have sung loudly, but they didn't win a single match and went home at the bottom of their group.

♪ ♩ NATIONAL EMOTION

Love for your country is called **patriotism**, and a national anthem is one expression of that feeling. Some countries are newer than others, and their anthems can be very emotional for fans. When Yugoslavia broke up into different states in 1991, countries such as Croatia, Slovenia, Macedonia, and Bosnia and Herzegovina were formed, with their own national anthems. The Bosnia and Herzegovina anthem has caused some problems: politicians in the country still have not been able to agree on the best lyrics to keep everyone happy, so it has no words at all. In some countries where there has been conflict, such as Rwanda and Iraq, anthems have been used to try to heal divisions.

Fans of newer countries tend to display their patriotism more and sing their anthems loud and proud. That's because when a country is newer, the people who live there tend to love it a bit more and want to show it off—like Ben does when he wears brand-new sneakers.

Whatever team you're following, we recommend that you support them by singing with gusto. The players will like it, and you will enjoy it too—even if your voice sounds like your granny screaming after she's stubbed her toe!

ALEX AND BEN'S SONGBOOK
TOP FIVE FAVORITE NATIONAL ANTHEMS

BY NAME:

1. Senegal – "Pluck Your Koras, Strike the Balafons"
2. Norway – "Yes, We Love This Country"
3. Bangladesh – "My Golden Bengal"
4. Honduras – "Your Flag Is a Heavenly Light"
5. Nepal – "Made of Hundreds of Flowers"

BY TUNE:

1. Italy – "The Song of the Italians"
2. Brazil – "Brazilian National Anthem"
3. France – "La Marseillaise"
4. Uruguay – "National Hymn"
5. United States – "The Star-Spangled Banner"

CHANTELLE RHYMES

☆ STAR
STUDENT

" Higher! "

☆☆ STAR
☆ STUDENT stats

Whispers before she sings:
"1-2-3-4"
Vocal range: 9 octaves
Top volume: 100 decibels
Beats per minute: 120
Birthplace: Singapore
Supports: Seattle Sounders
(United States)
Fave player: Alex Song
Trick: A master of the one-two

MUSIC QUIZ

1. **The Netherlands has the world's oldest national anthem. It is called:**

a) "Boring Tune"
b) "The Bit We Hum"
c) "Ta-Ra-Ra-Boom-De-Ay"
d) "The William"

2. **Which of the following is a line from the Real Madrid anthem "Hala Madrid"?**

a) "I wear your shirt right next to my heart!"
b) "We are called Real Madrid because we are real!"
c) "Madrid has the best restaurants in the world!"
d) "We love you more than we love life!"

3. **Which is the only country in the world to have a national anthem that was cowritten by its president?**

a) Kazakhstan
b) Bolivia
c) North Korea
d) Swaziland

4. **Which song by American pop legend Elvis Presley is sung by supporters of the MLS team the Portland Timbers at home games?**

a) "The Wonder of You"
b) "A Little Less Conversation"
c) "Can't Help Falling in Love"
d) "Heartbreak Hotel"

5. **What lyrics did Portuguese club Porto complain to UEFA about, after Manchester City fans made up a tune about their Brazilian forward Hulk?**

a) "You're not incredible!"
b) "You're green and you know you are!"
c) "Stand up if you smell Hulk!"
d) "Where is your Spider-Man?"

PHYSICS

Let's start our final lesson of the week with some bad news: we're all doomed!

The number of people on Earth is growing, and we are running out of space for homes and growing food. There will come a time when there is no room left.

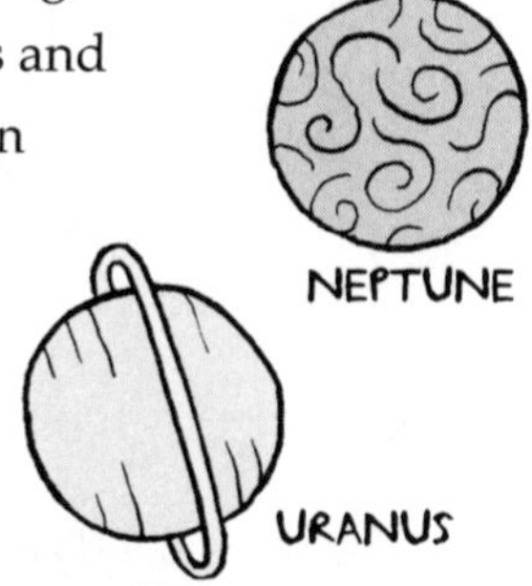

Now for the good news: there's a whole universe out there to explore.

We're going to leave Soccer School far behind and see if it is possible to play soccer on Mars.

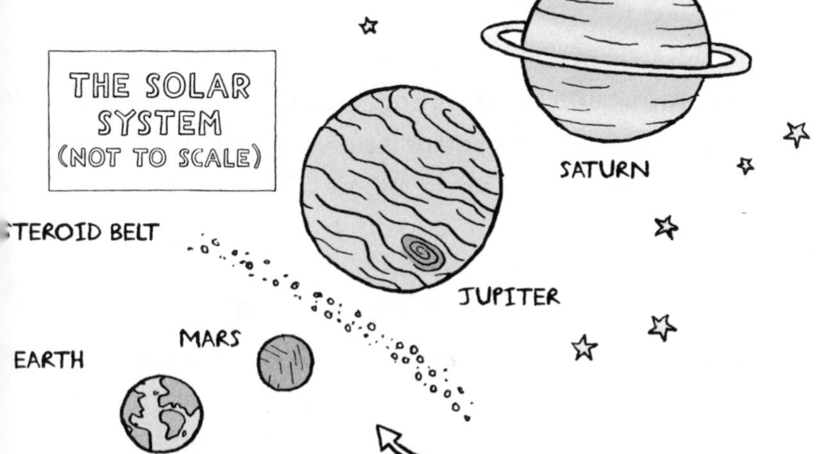

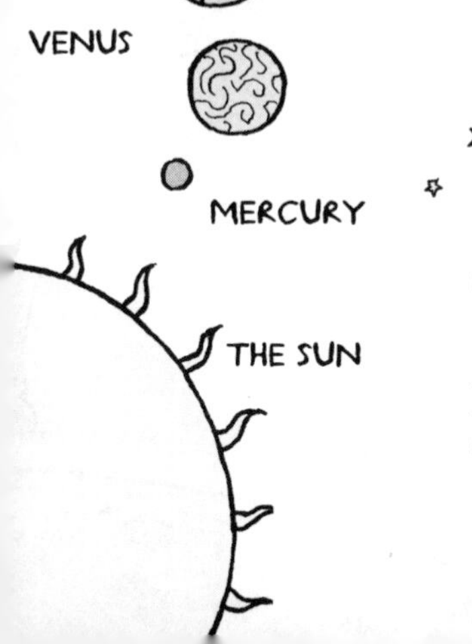

NEPTUNE

URANUS

THE SOLAR SYSTEM (NOT TO SCALE)

SATURN

ASTEROID BELT

JUPITER

EARTH

MARS

VENUS

MERCURY

THE SUN

Mars is the planet next to Earth in our solar system and the one scientists think is most suitable for human colonization.

Are you ready to visit the red planet? Five. Four. Three. Two. One. BLAST OFF!

COLD AND DARK

There are many challenges to living on Mars. First, it is butt-spankingly cold. The average temperature is about –76°F / –60°C, the same as in winter at the South Pole.

Second, there's not enough oxygen in the atmosphere. Humans need oxygen in order to breathe, so if we went outside on Mars, we would need to wear oxygen masks at all times.

Third, there is about half the amount of light as there is on Earth, since it is farther from the sun.

Still, these are only minor inconveniences and would not stop us from playing soccer—if not outside, then on floodlit indoor fields.

WHAT AN ATMOSPHERE

However, soccer on Mars would be a very different game from the one we enjoy on Earth. This is because of phenomena it's impossible to do anything about.

When you kick a ball on Mars, it will go much higher and travel much farther than when you kick one on Earth. This is for two reasons:

1. GRAVITY

The force that makes objects fall to the ground when you drop them is called **gravity**. The gravity on Mars is about a third of the gravity on Earth. This is mainly because Mars is a smaller and lighter planet than Earth.

If you drop a ball on Mars, it will fall to the ground more slowly than it would if you dropped it on Earth. So when you kick a ball on Mars, it will travel much farther before it lands than on Earth, as it is not being pulled down as quickly.

If you kick a ball upward on Mars, it will go much higher, too. When goalkeepers take a goal kick, they will easily shoot the ball out of the stadium.

The lower gravity will also mean that you can jump about three times higher than you could on Earth. This will make headers a lot more entertaining.

2. AIR RESISTANCE

Air is what we call the invisible gases that surround the earth. These gases—mostly nitrogen and oxygen—are made up of tiny **particles**. But what are particles? Wave your hand quickly in front of you, and you will feel a gust. That's the feeling of billions of particles hitting your hand. When a ball moves through air, it will also cause a gust. The air particles that are in the way of the ball slow it down. This effect is called **air resistance**.

There is also air on Mars—mostly a gas called carbon dioxide—but it is about a hundred times thinner than the air on Earth. In other words, the air on Mars has far fewer particles in it. A kicked ball will travel farther because there are fewer gas particles slowing it down.

☆ DON'T BEND IT LIKE . . .

The tiny amount of air resistance on Mars means that playing soccer will be different in another way, too: it will be impossible to bend the ball when you kick it. On Earth, in order to curve a free kick or a corner, you need to slice the ball so that it spins as it moves. The spinning ball hits the air particles, and this causes it to curve. But if you slice a ball on Mars, the spinning ball will not curve because there are not enough particles for it to hit. Players who are famous for curling their free kicks would stink on Mars.

FAMOUS
FREE-KICK TAKERS
David Beckham (England)
Ronald Koeman (Netherlands)
Siniša Mihajlović (Serbia)
Juninho Pernambucano (Brazil)
Andrea Pirlo (Italy)

SPACE SOCCER

So playing soccer on Mars will be a challenge. A future FMSA (Fédération Martien de Soccer Association) will have to decide whether to counter the problems by changing the rules of the game.

In order to make sure the ball does not travel such long distances, players will have to learn to kick it with less force than normal. Or the FMSA could introduce a much heavier, less bouncy ball. But these options might make games slow and boring to watch.

Another option for the FMSA would be to increase the size of the field so that players could kick the ball farther, but this might make it unpleasant for fans, who may need to bring binoculars to see what is going on.

Soccer can make the transition to Mars—but only time will tell if the Martians are going to enjoy it quite as much as we do on Earth now.

ANOTHER PLANET

Planets in the solar system that are more distant than Mars present even bigger challenges for soccer.

PLANET	MAIN PROBLEM	OUTCOME
Venus	860°F/460°C	Ball melts
Jupiter	No solid surface	Running on liquid
Neptune	Too windy	Ball flies away

VENUS SUPERNOVA

STAR STUDENT

"Cosmic!"

STAR STUDENT **stats**

Average jump: 10 ft./ 3 m
Thickness of soccer jersey:
   2 in./5 cm
Daily commute from Mars:
   8 months
Sock fluorescence: 500 units
Birthplace: Little Rock, Arkansas
Supports: LA Galaxy (United
   States)
Fave surface: Astroturf
☆ Trick: Hanging in the air

PHYSICS QUIZ

1. **Which planet is closest to the sun?**

a) Saturn
b) Mercury
c) Venus
d) Jupiter

2. **What does gravity explain?**

a) Why this book falls to the floor when you drop it
b) Why nails stick to a magnet
c) Why you can't breathe on Mars
d) Why gravy is delicious

3. **Why is Mars known as the red planet?**

a) The person who discovered it supported Manchester United.
b) It is very hot.
c) It is covered with red dust.
d) It used to be called Red Land.

4. **Which U.S. team did English midfielder David Beckham play for?**

a) New York Cosmos
b) Houston Dynamo
c) LA Galaxy
d) Colorado Comets

5. **Which recently discovered galaxy was named after a soccer player?**

a) Red Star 7, named after Raheem Sterling
b) Cosmos Redshift 7, named after Cristiano Ronaldo
c) Luminous Meteor 9, named after Lionel Messi
d) Novo Golaço 9, named after Neymar

QUIZ ANSWERS

BIOLOGY (9)
1. d
2. b
3. b
4. c
5. d

ENGLISH (21)
1. c
2. d
3. b
4. c
5. c

MATH (31)
1. a
2. c
3. c
4. a
5. b

ZOOLOGY (43)
1. c
2. a
3. c, dragon
4. a
5. b

PHYS. ED. (55)
1. b
2. a
3. b
4. c
5. a

HISTORY (67)
1. b
2. c
3. c
4. a
5. a

PSYCHOLOGY (77)
1. b
2. b
3. b
4. c
5. b

DESIGN TECHNOLOGY (87)
1. c
2. d
3. b
4. a
5. c

GEOGRAPHY (99)
1. b
2. a
3. d
4. c
5. d

DRAMA (109)
1. a
2. a
3. b
4. c
5. a

PHILOSOPHY (121)
1. a
2. a
3. c
4. c
5. a

PHOTOGRAPHY (133)
1. a
2. c
3. c
4. b
5. c

BUSINESS STUDIES (143)
1. d
2. b
3. d c a b
4. a
5. d

FASHION (153)
1. b
2. b
3. d
4. c
5. a

COMPUTER SCIENCE (163)
1. d
2. c
3. b
4. a
5. d

POLITICAL SCIENCE (175)
1. c
2. c
3. a
4. a
5. c

MUSIC (185)
1. d
2. a
3. a
4. c
5. a

PHYSICS (193)
1. b
2. a
3. c
4. c
5. b

ACKNOWLEDGMENTS

All the best teams need support from other people. We were thrilled to have illustrator Spike Gerrell as our teammate. Spike, you are a genius.

We were lucky that friends, family, and experts were happy to contribute to *Soccer School* in many different ways. Our agents, Rebecca Carter and David Luxton, always offered the right advice and encouragement.

We couldn't have wished for a more enthusiastic, dedicated, and creative squad at Walker Books. There's only one Denise Johnstone-Burt, Daisy Jellicoe, Iree Pugh, Louise Jackson, and Alice Primmer!

We would like to thank the following for their time and expertise: Peter Alegi, Alan Ames, Tim Angel, David Barber, Rosa Bransky, Ciaran Brennan, Razvan Burleanu, Greg Cohen, Pete Etchells, Dion Fanning, Ian Forgacs, Tai Foster, James Hartnett, Eagle Heights, Stephen Hunt, Leigh Ireland, Miles Jacobson, Professor David James, Tom Jenkins, Simon Kuper, Andrew Lawn, Steve Lawrence, Mark Lyttleton, Robert MacNeice, Alex Marshall, Steve McNally, Don McPherson, Mark Miodownik, James Montague, Ben Oakley, Sarah Oakley, Sam Pilger, Josh Rattet, Adam Rutherford, Richard Sadlier, David Spiegelhalter, Alan Spurgeon, Luis Vidigal, and David Winner.

Thanks to our original Star Students: Dylan Auerbach, Joe Baden-Powell, Rafi and Zak Bartfeld, Maya and Joshie Greenslade, Thibaut Lyttleton, and Saul and Gabriel Pardon.

Alex would like to thank Ruth Shurman and Roman Pardon for helping with the germination of the idea. He couldn't have done it without Natalie's love and encouragement and Zak's early-morning wake-up calls.

Ben would like to thank Annie for her inspiration and support, and Clemmy and Bibi, the sweetest proofreaders anyone could wish for.

ABOUT YOUR COACHES

Alex Bellos writes for the *Guardian*. He has written several best-selling popular-science books and created two mathematical coloring books. He loves puzzles.

Ben Lyttleton is a journalist, broadcaster, and soccer consultant. He has written books about how to score the perfect penalty and what we can learn from soccer's best managers.

Spike Gerrell grew up loving both playing soccer and drawing pictures. He now gets to draw for a living. At heart, though, he will always be a central midfielder.

ENJOY THIS SNEAK PEEK AT SEASON TWO OF SOCCER SCHOOL!

Coming soon!

Find out more at
www.soccerschoolseries.com

Find Soccer School
on YouTube at
www.youtube.com/c/
FootballSchoolFacts